W9-BFU-260

SYSTEMATIC DATA COLLECTION

WITHDRAWN
FROM
UNIVERSITY OF PENNSYLVANIA
LIBRARIES

SUSAN C. WELLER
University of Pennsylvania
A. KIMBALL ROMNEY
University of California, Irvine

Qualitative Research Methods,
Volume 10

SAGE PUBLICATIONS
The International Professional Publishers
Newbury Park London New Delhi

Copyright © 1988 by Sage Publications, Inc.

All rights reserved. No part of this book may be reproduced or utilized in any form or by any means, electronic or mechanical, including photocopying, recording, or by any information storage and retrieval system, without permission in writing from the publisher.

For information address:

SAGE Publications, Inc.
2455 Teller Road
Newbury Park, California 91320
E-mail: order@sagepub.com

SAGE Publications Ltd.
6 Bonhill Street
London EC2A 4PU
United Kingdom

SAGE Publications India Pvt. Ltd.
M-32 Market
Greater Kailash I
New Delhi 110 048 India

ANNENBERG
RESERVE
H
62
W415
1988

Printed in the United States of America

Library of Congress Cataloging-in-Publication Data

Weller, Susan C.
Systematic data collection.

(Qualitative research methods; v. 10)
Bibliography: p.
1. Social sciences—Field work. 2. Social Sciences—Research. 3. Interviewing. I. Romney, A. Kimball (Antone Kimball). II. Title. III. Series.
H62.W415 1987 300′.723 87-23475
ISBN 0-8039-3073-9
ISBN 0-8039-3074-7 (pbk.)

98 99 00 01 12 11 10 9 8

CONTENTS

EDITORS' INTRODUCTION

To many, ethnography conjures stereotypes of field researchers dutifully laboring to make holistic sense of a complex world, attempting to notice and record all things important in culture. Because the mission is impossible, ethnographic compromises take the form of copious field observations, verbatim accounts, and general impressions. The good news of working in this time-honored, if unstructured, way has received regular treatment in the *Qualitative Research Methods Series.* The bad news, of course, is that ethnographers have too often discovered too late that the value of their interview information is discounted as a consequence of poor sampling (of questions, of informants) and poor elicitation techniques.

In this tenth monograph of the *Series*, Susan C. Weller and A. Kimball Romney show how systematic interviewing complements traditional ethnographic practices. The authors describe in detail how to settle on a research domain of interest, how to form culturally meaningful questions, how to choose a data collection method from an impressive array of alternatives, and how to tally responses to generate desirable (e.g., ordered, similarity, test performance) data types. Weller and Romney justify these strategies with an especially useful discussion of reliability and validity.

The structure that Weller and Romney bring to interviewing is of the right kind. The volume compels field researchers to take very seriously not only what they hear, but what they ask. The ethnographic result is bound to be better science.

—Marc L. Miller
John Van Maanen
Peter K. Manning

SYSTEMATIC DATA COLLECTION

SUSAN C. WELLER
University of Pennsylvania

A. KIMBALL ROMNEY
University of California, Irvine

1. INTRODUCTION TO STRUCTURED INTERVIEWING

This book is designed to help students and researchers in the social sciences collect better interview or questionnaire data. We hope to do this by providing directions for using a variety of formats for the collection of such data. Our discussion is limited to systematic interviewing where each informant is asked the same set of questions. This excludes many kinds of very valuable interviewing procedures such as the genealogical method of Rivers (1910) and clinical interviewing in psychology and psychiatry. We also exclude the collection of response data elicited by open-ended questions that need to be coded, categorized, or reworked by the researcher.

There is a large literature on various forms of open-ended interviewing where subjects are asked to give long explanatory answers to a variety of questions. These forms of interviewing are very valuable in many kinds of research and in the beginning stages of more formal investigations. In this book, however, we restrict ourselves to questions and tasks that are asked in such a way that informants' responses and informants' categories are elicited and used directly. These procedures help avoid researcher bias resulting from imposing a priori categories that may not correspond to those of the people being studied.

The social and behavioral sciences, like all sciences, depend upon experimental and observational data as the "raw material" for increased understanding. Such understanding, the ultimate goal of all sciences, requires the careful analysis of observations to assess their relationship to currently accepted knowledge. Major advances in our understanding usually require systematic observation, classification, interpretation, and study over a period of time. It is our hope that the wider use of structured interviewing formats provided in this book would improve the quality of much of the "raw material" in the social sciences.

The gathering of data is only the first step in the quest for understanding; data must then be analyzed and interpreted with the aid of theory. The task of theory is to develop models for the processes that underlie phenomena. Theories facilitate the calculation of properties of the models. Observations or experimental results can then be compared to model properties. When such comparisons are favorable and the predictions accurate, understanding is advanced. The increased use of structured formats should aid in this overall task of understanding human behavior.

At the beginning of any social science study involving the collection of interview data the researcher is faced with the problem of what questions to ask and what is the best format for the phrasing of questions. Different data collection techniques are appropriate during different stages of research. In the beginning stages, informal exploratory interviewing is necessary in order to define the area of inquiry and obtain a general notion of what to expect. Later, formal methods are appropriate in order to measure accurately the phenomena under consideration.

There recently has been a good deal of discussion in the social sciences about the relative merits of data collected through interviewing and talking to informants as compared to observing subjects in natural or experimental settings. Some have gone so far as to suggest that people are not capable of providing good data through verbal reports. We believe that this issue is frequently distorted and misunderstood. Using the various methods for collecting data presented in this book, reliable and valid results can be produced routinely. The accuracy of the results are not generally appreciated. With reasonable care reliability figures above .95 are easily possible. Various studies of validity demonstrate that equally high results are reasonable to expect. Specific evidence will be presented in the final chapters of the book.

An important issue that needs to be discussed is how the choice of a data collection method depends upon the type of data desired. Data type is not necessarily a function of the data collection format; it is frequently determined by the type of question that is asked and how responses are tabulated. Therefore, we would like to present the data collection methods as somewhat independent of the kind of data produced. This book is organized by method and the different "types" of data that can be obtained from each method are discussed in each chapter. Data types that are referred to include: similarity data, ordered data, and test performance data. Similarity data consist of informants' judged similarity estimates among study items. Ordered data consist of an ordinal ranking (or rating) of items on a single conceptual scale. Performance data refer to responses that can be graded as "correct" or "incorrect."

Plan of the Book

In the following chapters we describe the use of various formats for the collection of data in structured interviewing and paper-and-pencil questionnaires. In each chapter we discuss the method in general and then give detailed step-by-step directions for its use. We also give examples of the use of each of the methods as well as summarize their strengths and weaknesses.

We begin, in Chapter 2, by describing the procedures for finding how respondents define the boundaries of a given subject matter or domain of interest. Chapters 3 and 4 discuss the use of the pile sort as a useful format for obtaining judged similarity among a large number of objects. The pile sort is a format in which the subject is asked to sort items into piles so that objects within piles are more similar to each other than to objects in the other piles. Chapter 5 presents the method of triads. In the triad task the informant is presented with three items at a time and typically picks the one most different from the other two. Triads may be used to collect either similarity or ordered data. Rating scales, one of the most varied and widely used methods in the social sciences, are discussed in Chapter 6. Rating scales may be used to collect ordered data or to collect similarity data on pairs of items. Rank order tasks are described in Chapter 7. Chapter 8 provides a complete description and explanation of balanced incomplete block designs that may be used to shorten and simplify triad, paired comparison, and ranking tasks. We devote Chapter 9 to a discussion of the use of sentence frames as a systematic interviewing technique that is especially useful where the items in a domain are characterized by a variety of features. In Chapter 10 we discuss a variety of other data collection formats. These include true-false questions, multiple-choice questions, fill-in-the-blank questions, matching designs, direct estimation, and "pick n" items from an array. In the last two chapters we discuss reliability and validity. We illustrate various ways in which confidence in the results from interviewing can be increased by using such techniques as replication and the convergence of results from different methods.

Although this book is addressed primarily to social scientists, it is appropriate for anyone who wants to study attitudes and beliefs. While a political scientist may want to use a technique to study how particular political candidates are perceived, a market researcher may use the same techniques to study preferences for different brands of cigarettes. Similarly, one sociologist may use structured interviewing techniques to study perceptions of occupational prestige, while another may study social networks. Anthropologists working with nonliterates may be particularly interested in the oral data collection methods. While we cannot review all the possible applications, we would like to note that the interviewing and data collection tasks contained in this volume are as appropriate for use in such exotic settings as the highlands of New Guinea as they are in the corporate offices on Wall Street. It is our expectation that the book will provide the researcher with a larger choice of data collection techniques than has been heretofore available in a single place.

2. DEFINING A DOMAIN AND FREE LISTING

The first step in any study is to obtain a clear understanding of the definition and boundaries of what is being studied. Since this book is about interviewing there is an implicit assumption that the researcher is interested in what the respondents think about "something." For convenience we call the "something" a semantic or cultural domain. The semantic or cultural domain is simply the subject matter of interest, a set of related items. Examples of domains that have been studied include color terms, kinship terms, diseases, plant terms, animal terms, airplane piloting errors, kinds of pain, and characteristics of infant feeding methods. The concept of a domain is a very general one and may include almost any coherently defined subject matter.

A domain may be defined as an organized set of words, concepts, or sentences, all on the same level of contrast, that jointly refer to a single conceptual sphere. The items in a domain derive their meanings, in part, from their position in a mutually interdependent system reflecting the way in which a given language or culture classifies the relevant conceptual sphere. For example, the concept of "shape," may have category members such as "round," "square," "rectangular," and so on. Each of these is a kind of shape and each says something different about shape. We refer to "shape" as the generic name of the category and the words "round" and the like as items or objects in the domain.

The overall success of any study depends in part on giving careful attention to the definition of the domain as the first step of the research. Generally the domain should be defined by the informants, in their language, and not by the investigator. It is easy to assume falsely that the investigator knows the domain and can therefore define what items belong in the domain and what items do not belong in the domain. If researchers want to study beliefs about discipline in different ethnic groups, it is only after disciplinary actions and punishments are explicitly listed that it is appropriate to worry about the format and design of the interview instrument. The immediate problem is to specify which disciplinary actions and punishments should be included in the interview.

There are many ways to compile a list of items to define the domain of study items. On rare occasions there may be an absolute definition. The alphabet, the Morse code, the names of the months, the days of the week, presidents of the United States, and the states of the United States are all examples of a priori defined domains. Usually, however, the investigator does not know the boundaries of the domain and needs some sort of elicitation procedure to ensure that the investigator's definition of the domain corresponds to that of the informants.

The most useful general technique for isolating and defining a domain is the free listing task. The use of free listing as an elicitation technique has several useful applications. Perhaps its most important use is to ensure that one is dealing with culturally relevant items and to delineate the boundaries of a semantic or cultural domain. The free listing task can also be used to study or make inferences about informants' cognitive structure from the order of recall, the frequency of recall, and the use of modifiers (Romney and D'Andrade, 1964).

Requests such as "Name all the x's that you know" or "What kinds of x's are there" can elicit domain items. For example, in a comparative study of disease concepts a free list task was used by Weller (1984a: 342):

> To ensure that culturally relevant items would be used, 20 women in each country were asked to name all the illnesses they could think of and to describe each. Using the most frequently mentioned items, a domain of 29 English and 27 Spanish disease terms was selected . . . and used in the subsequent data collection tasks.

There are several things that can be observed and inferred from such lists. First, some items are more "salient," "better known," "important," or "familiar" than other items, and such items occur earlier or higher up in an individual's list than those that lack such characteristics. Second, there is usually a great range in the number of people that mentioned each item. Thus we can think of two different indices of "saliency." The first is the position of an item on a list and the second is the proportion of the lists on which the item appears. These two indices tend to be highly correlated. For example, Romney and D'Andrade (1964: 155) report a correlation of .83 between these two indices for 105 free lists of "kinds of relatives." These indicators of salience also are closely related to the frequency of usage of each item in ordinary language as measured in the Thorndike-Lorge (1944) word list. Free lists, when drawn from fairly large samples (such as 100 or more) provide similar information.

Many domains contain far more elements than are practical to include in a single interview instrument. This adds the complication of sampling items from the domain for inclusion in the interview. The free listing task allows us to find the most salient items with minimal effort. Items that do not appear on the lists are probably not as common or salient as items that do appear. The list is not to be taken as definitive and complete. If we interviewed additional informants we might increase the number of items. However, as the number of informants increases, the list becomes stable and the order of items tends not to change as few new items are added by each new person.

How to Do It

We would like to emphasize the importance of defining the domain of items for study as a first step prior to the use of other systematic data collection techniques. Domain definition, whether done with a free list or variation on the free list, is extremely important and assures that the domain is defined by the informants in their language. Without free listing the items may reflect the ideas of the researcher rather than the informants. This step is so important that we suggest that it not be omitted or delegated.

What to ask. The first step in obtaining items for study is to decide upon a domain, for example, illnesses, cars, colors, kin terms. The next step is to decide on how to ask informants to list the items. Getting the right question can be difficult, although on occasion it is easy.

To find out if the question is productive it is necessary to pretest the wording. By trying the wording on four or five people it is generally possible to tell if the question is appropriate. When one has the right wording, the interview flows smoothly, the informant understands the question and produces reasonable items at reasonable frequencies. Sometimes informants respond with too few items. In such cases, the question wording might need to be changed. Sometimes informants are not used to responding to questions with lists of items and probes may be useful. For example, "You said that _____ and _____ are ways to treat malaria. What other ways are there for treating malaria?" Do not ask *if* there are any other treatments, ask *what* other treatments there are. Open ended questions that can be answered with a yes or no are too often answered with a no.

If the problem lies with the question you are asking, you need to try asking the question in new ways. It is possible that what the researcher thinks is a domain is not a domain for the informants. Rephrase the question and talk with the informants until a question is found that makes sense. In some cases it helps to elicit statements rather than words. Instead of asking "List kinds of health care" it is possible to ask "What did you like about the health care you received? What were the things that you did not like? What things do you wish you had gotten?" Responses should be recorded verbatim.

It is important to encourage the informants to clarify their responses. Do not assume that you know what the respondent means, ask for further explanation. For example, when Weller and Dungy (1986) asked about the advantages of breast feeding, one woman responded that it was convenient. That statement sounds clear. We think we know what it means, but what exactly is meant by convenient? As it turns out, "convenient" means something different to breast and bottle feeders. To the breast feeders it means that they can feed their baby without the hassle of preparing bottles. To bottle feeders it means that they can feed their baby anywhere without embarrassment.

Variations on what to ask. The choice of which questions to use in eliciting the free lists is sometimes fairly straightforward. However, in many cases there is no obvious single question to elicit domain items and variations in approach are useful. Sometimes just asking for a free listing does not elicit very long lists. In some of these situations a modified type of free listing task can be used to elicit descriptive phrases for further study. For example, Romney et al. (1979), in attempting to identify and measure attributes of success and failure, asked respondents to list five friends and characterize the ways in which each was successful and the ways in which each might be considered a failure. Respondents were encouraged to use their own definitions of success and failure.

Combining more than one kind of list is another possibility. For example, in seeking the reasons why women choose to breast or bottle feed, Weller and Dungy (1986) asked each woman to list (1) the advantages of breastfeeding, (2) the disadvantages of breastfeeding, (3) the advantages of bottlefeeding, and (4) the disadvantages of bottlefeeding. All four lists were combined to form the domain of "the characteristics of feeding methods."

Another kind of variation on free listing is the use of "contrasting questions." Young (1980) wanted to elicit reasons given by Mexican Indian villagers for choosing one source of medical care over another. He first obtained a list of all sources of health care in the village. He then presented the informants with *pairs* of alternative sources of health care. The format of his questions was "Why/when would you go to ________ instead of ________?" In this way he was able to construct a list of reasons for choosing one medical care over another. Krackhardt and Kilduff (1987) presented items in sets of three, asked informants to choose the most similar pair, and asked informants to explain why those items were similar.

Sometimes it is useful to work with two related lists, for example, to elicit disease terms and then elicit symptoms and causes of each disease. This technique was used by Weller et al. (1987). In initial interviews, adolescents were asked to list things they could "do wrong." Probes included asking about things that their friends or anyone else had done wrong. Then after listing all the things possible, each person was asked, for each of the misbehaviors, to name all of the things that their parents or some other adult might do in response as punishment. Thus for each misbehavior an additional list was obtained, namely, a list of possible parental punishments.

Free lists also can be combined with information from other sources. For example, in the study of "discipline" discussed above the authors wanted to include some "abusive" forms of punishments to see if there were differences between Anglo and Mexican American perceptions of the acceptability of those punishments. Not surprisingly, the free lists did not include extremely harsh parental responses. To ensure that the final list did include some harsh punishments, the researchers obtained a list of the most frequently reported cases of physical abuse seen in the Pediatric Emergency Room at the University Hospital. They added these to round out the final list.

Berlin and Romney (1964), in attempting to find all the numeral classifiers in Tzeltal, used a clever way of eliciting all members of a semantic domain. By depending upon informant recall and other informal methods they isolated a few dozen numerical classifiers. Since all of them had the form CVC (Consonant, Vowel, Consonant) they were then able to generate, with the help of a computer, all possible combinations of Tzeltal consonants and vowels of the appropriate form. There were 4,410 such possible combinations. By presenting each of the forms independently to two informants they were able to isolate 557 numeral classifiers: "This number is considerably greater than any other inventory thus far published. Without the systematic eliciting procedures described above, less than a tenth of the classifiers in Tzeltal would have been discovered, for their actual occurrence in textual material is infrequent. The list may not be complete, but it approaches the full inventory" (1964: 81).

Group interviews (nominal group process, Delphi groups, focused group interviews) are also sometimes used to establish a list of items of interest. Nominal and Delphi groups usually begin with a group leader requesting that each participant write down all of their feelings, reasons, or concerns regarding the topic of discussion. For example, if the group is assembled to discuss student evaluations, then they might be asked to list all of the ways in which a student might be properly evaluated. If the group has been assembled by the vice president of a major car manufacturing company, they might be asked to list all the features that the next new model car should have. The group process begins as each person is asked to contribute one or two items to a master "group" list. When the master list contains most or all of the items from the initial lists, then participants are asked to choose the most important items. The group process continues with individuals discussing the listed options with the goal of obtaining a single consensual list.

Data can be used from nominal or Delphi groups if the following things are kept in mind. First, the sample size is not the number of participants in a group, rather it is the number of groups. If the initial lists are collected prior to discussion, the number of respondents would be equal to the number of participants in the group. After discussion and interaction, however, the data from individual lists are no longer independent and the group, in effect, becomes an individual in terms of generating items.

Minimum number of informants needed. Usually with a coherent domain, 20 to 30 informants are sufficient. Larger or smaller numbers of informants are necessary depending upon the amount of agreement in the responses. Of course 10 informants at this stage are better than no informants. If one keeps track of the frequencies in a sequential way it is possible to tell when stability in order is reached and use this as a guide for how many informants are necessary. To illustrate, Weller (1980) cumulatively tabulated lists and examined the order and frequency of items. Since the relative order of frequencies of items (see Tabulation below) did not change, and few new items were added by increasing the sample size from 10 to 15 and from 15 to 20, a sample size of 20 was assumed to be adequate.

Tabulation

Responses are tabulated by counting the number of respondents that mentioned each item. Items are then ordered in terms of frequency of response as in Tables 2.1 and 2.2. The tabulated list of items is a frequency distribution of the number of respondents that mentioned each item. Frequencies can be re-expressed as percentages where desirable. Frequencies or percentages may be used as estimates of how salient or important each item is to the sample of informants.

It is important to note that when multiple questions are asked of a single informant, responses should be tabulated by the number of persons mentioning each item and not the total number of times that an item is mentioned. With multiple-related questions an informant may give the same response more than once. When this occurs it is important to count that response only once for that informant. The frequency distribution of the tabulated items should always reflect the number of persons that mentioned the item.

The final tabulated list of items can sometimes be diagnostic of whether or not the researcher asked a meaningful question. If items are arranged in order of their frequency of mention, with the most frequently mentioned items at the top of the list, the top item probably will have been mentioned by a majority of the sample (say 75%). Frequencies should then descend slowly, dribbling down to the lowest frequency (say, to the twentieth or fiftieth item that was mentioned only once). If instead, only the top two or three items were mentioned by a majority and the frequencies drop off sharply, that indicates (1) the domain is small (i.e., has only a few members) or, more likely, (2) the researcher did not use adequate probes and encouragements with informants, or (3) the researcher did not ask about a coherent domain.

Coding and standardization of responses. When the lists consist of phrases or statements rather than words it is common for each list to contain different phrasings of the same concept. Here, in tabulating the lists the researcher will have to use judgment as to which statements refer to the "same" concepts. The researcher also has to use judgment as to the best phrasing of each concept. The goal is to collect and tabulate verbatim responses, not to try and infer categories. When making categories for responses, the researcher runs the risk that the categories will reflect his or her own preconceived notions and biases and not the ideas of the informants. (To collect data on the categories used by your informants, refer to Chapters 3 and 5.) In difficult cases it would be desirable to seek the aid of informants in deciding when two different phrases represent a single concept.

The following criteria for standardizing statements are suggested as generally useful: use correct grammar and speech; make each statement autonomous and clear (e.g., the sentence "He works hard at it," should be rewritten as "He works hard at his job."); use present tense; avoid specific words and phrases where possible (e.g., use the word *car* rather than *Ford,* unless it changes the meaning).

What items should be included in the final study. The decision of how many items to use is determined by a number of considerations including: the purpose of the study, the number and frequency of the items elicited in the free listing, and the type of formal data collection format to be used. Clearly, the most frequently named items should be given top priority. Where to draw the cutoff point is more difficult to specify. Generally the domain is too large to allow consideration of every item and therefore the items to be studied are a sample of the whole. Sometimes low-frequency items are included to ensure variety of objects. There are no absolute rules for inclusion and exclusion of items. For many purposes a couple dozen items seems reasonable while for others larger samples of items may be required. The researcher should be sure that items included in the study domain *are known* by the vast majority of the informants. Otherwise the results can be severely biased by informants who are not acquainted with the items.

Strengths and Weaknesses of Free Listing

We recommend free listing as the first step in all research involving the definition of new domains. Free listing is the best way to ensure that the concepts and the domain are culturally relevant. It provides a strong source of cognitive data in terms of frequencies and the order properties of the individual lists. Informants can usually do the task in an easy and natural way. Free listing helps prevent researchers from using inappropriate items.

Free listing, however, is not a perfect tool. Sometimes it is difficult to find appropriate generic terms to start the listing process or lists may not be productive (lists are too sparse). Finally, there are no generally recognized ways to check the statistical reliability of the free listing task.

An Example

In order to illustrate the use of the free listing task, we present the results of a classroom exercise using the domains of "fruits" and "vegetables" to illustrate problems of defining boundaries between domains. The question arose as to whether the two domains were absolutely separate or whether they might overlap somewhat in membership. In order to get a preliminary idea of the relation of the two domains we asked 40 students to "List the names of all the fruits that you can." We asked a different set of 60 students to "List the names of all the vegetables that you can."

The results of the free listing tasks are shown in Tables 2.1 and 2.2. Table 2.1 shows the number of times each fruit was mentioned. The

TABLE 2.1
Frequency of Mention of "Fruits" in Free List Task

Apple	37	Honeydew	9
Orange	35	*Avocado	8
Pear	34	Mango	8
Banana	33	Date	7
Grape	32	Fig	7
Peach	30	Prune	7
Tangerine	27	Gooseberry	6
Cherry	26	Raisin	5
Grapefruit	26	*Pumpkin	4
Pineapple	26	Casaba melon	3
Strawberry	22	Kumquat	3
Watermelon	21	Melon	3
Lemon	20	Breadfruit	2
*Tomato	19	Kiwi	2
Apricot	18	Passionfruit	2
Blueberry	18	Persimmon	2
Plum	18	Cranberry	1
Cantaloupe	17	Crenshaw melon	1
Lime	16	Currant	1
Nectarine	14	Elderberry	1
Papaya	14	Huckleberry	1
Raspberry	14	Loganberry	1
Blackberry	13	Manderine	1
Boisenberry	12	*Rhubarb	1
Tangello	11	Salmonberry	1
Guava	10	*Squash	1
Pomegranate	10	Taro	1
Coconut	9	Turnip	1

fruits are ordered from the most frequently mentioned to those that were mentioned only once. Table 2.2 shows the same data for vegetables. Note that there is a great range in the number of people that mentioned each fruit. For example, "apple" appears on 37 of the lists (about 93% of the respondents) and "taro" only appears on one list. This is typical of results from the free listing task. The question arises as to whether or not big differences in the proportion of times items are mentioned has any significance. We feel that it has great significance.

Notice that if we asked additional informants to list all the fruits that they knew that we might increase the number of items on the list in Table 2.1. Therefore the list is not to be taken as definitive and complete. The fruits that are not on the list are probably not as common or salient in these students' conceptions as are the fruits on the list. Notice that as the number of subjects increases we expect the list to become more stable, the order would not change, and few items would be added by each new subject.

TABLE 2.2
Frequency Distribution of "Vegetables" Free Listing Task

Green beans	55	Chinese peas	6
Corn	50	Greens	6
Carrots	49	Okra	6
Peas	41	Summer squash	6
Lima beans	40	Blackeyed peas	5
Lettuce	38	Swiss chard	5
Broccoli	37	Wax beans	5
Califlower	36	Bamboo shoots	4
Brussels sprouts	35	Navy beans	4
*Tomatoes	32	Alfalfa sprouts	3
Onions	30	Chile peppers	3
Spinach	30	Endive	3
Asparagus	29	Kidney beans	3
*Squash	28	Leek	3
Cucumbers	26	Parsnips	3
Celery	25	*Pumpkin	3
Cabbage	24	Redleaf lettuce	3
Zucchini	24	*Rhubarb	3
*Turnips	23	Water chestnuts	3
Potatoes	20	Butterleaf lettuce	2
Artichokes	18	Green onions	2
Bell peppers	18	Kale	2
Radishes	18	Kolari	2
*Avocado	18	Red onions	2
Beets	13	Sauerkraut	2
Rutabaga	11	Butternut squash	1
Bean sprouts	10	Garlic	1
Eggplant	9	Hubbard squash	1
Mushrooms	8	Jicama	1
Parsley	8	Peapods	1
Pinto beans	8	Pickles	1
Yams	7	Soybeans	1

*Indicates items that appear on both "fruit" and "vegetable" lists.

We can see from the lists that the two domains are not mutually exclusive. Six words occur on both lists. "Tomato" and "Avocado" appear frequently on both lists, while "Squash" and "Turnip" are more often seen as vegetables. In order to decide which list the items belong to we would need more information for "Pumpkin" and "Rhubarb." We might suspect that "Squash" and "Turnip" were really vegetables and that one person may have "made a mistake."

Where should we draw a line between the two domains? This is a matter of judgment and is usually based on the free list results. In this case, tomato and avocado might be assigned to both fruits and vegetables. In order to give an intuitive and visual answer to this kind of

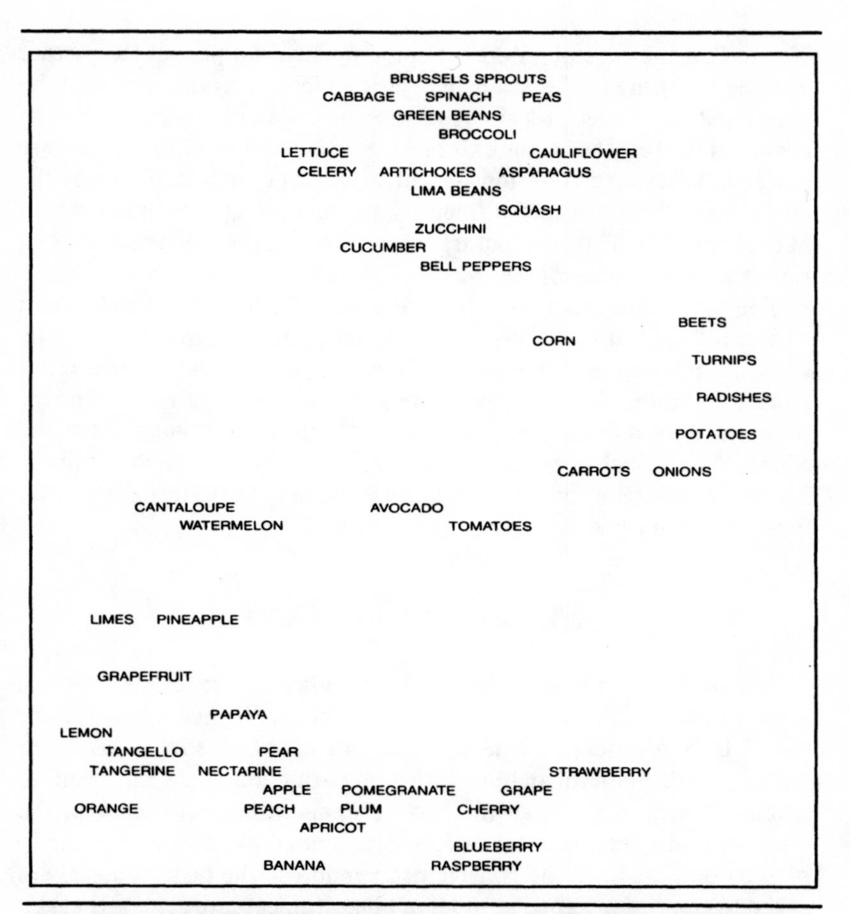

Figure 2.1: Judged Similarities Among Fruits and Vegetables Displayed in a Spatial Representation

situation we conducted further data collection and analysis and obtained a spatial representation of the more common fruits and vegetables in terms of their similarity. Although such an analysis is not necessary to define domain items, we present the results to illustrate the overlap between two domains and also to show kinds of results that can be obtained from structured interviewing. Students were asked to sort the names of fruits and vegetables into piles (see Chapter 3 for details). From the resulting judged similarity data we performed a multidimensional scaling analysis to obtain a spatial representation. Figure 2.1 shows the results. In this picture, items that were judged similar are close to each other while items judged as dissimilar are further apart. Closeness in the picture represents closeness in the similarity judgments.

Notice that the vegetables are all in the upper-right part of the picture and the fruits are in the lower part of the picture. Notice also that the root vegetables (beets, turnips, radishes, potatoes, onions, and carrots) are clustered together at the extreme right of the picture. Fruits that are berries are clustered at the lower right. A further cluster is formed by the citrus fruits (limes, grapefruit, lemon, tangello, tangerine, and orange) at the lower left. Thus the picture seems to represent similarities among the items in an interpretable way.

The main thing to notice from Figure 2.1 is that "Avocado" and "Tomato" are found exactly in the middle of the two groups. It can be seen that the two are intermediate between the two dense clusters that constitute "pure" fruits or "pure" vegetables. The cognitive boundary between fruits and vegetables is not a sharp all-or-none type distinction. Some items in each domain are more typical of the domain than others. The boundaries are somewhat arbitrary and may be defined differently for different purposes.

3. PILE SORT I: SINGLE SORTS

We turn now to more formal data collection methods that are appropriate when study items have been selected. We begin with sorting tasks. In a *pile sort* task informants are asked to sort cards, each containing the name of an item, into piles so that items in a pile are more similar to each other than they are to items in separate piles. In the unconstrained version of the task, subjects can make as few or as many piles as they wish. In the constrained version of the task, subjects are asked to create a specified number of piles. Subjects are generally asked to group items according to their similarity, without reference to specific criteria. The informant, rather than the researcher, decides what criteria are most salient and determine similarity. The pile sort is very easy to administer and allows for the collection of data among a large number of items.

Examples

The pile sorting task has been used extensively in field research. It is easy to use, respondents understand what is going on, and it can facilitate conversation. Miller and Johnson (1981) and Johnson and Miller (1983) used the pile sort to collect data on relations among fishermen. The task was quick, easy (some data was collected on the deck of a fishing boat while out at sea), and the men tended to talk about the social relations among the men that were being studied. When names or descriptive phrases of objects are used on cards the task is limited to literate informants. In cases where it is possible to use the actual objects themselves, or reasonable pictures, the method can be extended to nonliterate informants.

In a series of ethnographic studies, Roberts and associates have used the pile sort to facilitate the description of relevant behavior events for a number of diverse culture patterns, such as eight ball pool (Roberts and Chick, 1979), pilot error (Roberts et al., 1980), women's trapshooting (Roberts and Nuttras, 1980), and tennis (Roberts et al., 1981). For example, using a combination of participant observation and structured interviewing, Roberts et al. (1980) explored kinds of errors P-3 pilots can make. Errors that were known to have occurred and that represented the major types of errors were selected for study. Pilots were then asked to sort 60 such errors into piles according to their similarity. After the sorting task, they were asked to rate the errors in terms of their severity. Hierarchical clustering and multidimensional scaling were used to uncover the categories and dimensions of error.

In another application of the pile sort, Freeman et al. (1981) and Romney et al. (1979) compared concepts of success and failure in the United States with those in Guatemala. They selected representative statements of characteristics of success and failure. Examples of some of the U.S. success statements were the following: "He's ambitious," "Everything works out for him and always for the good," "He's stable," and " Always there when he's supposed to be." Examples of failures were the following: "He drinks too much," "He seems to want things for free," and "He feels he has to cheat to get ahead." Judged similarity data was collected with a pile sorting task:

> Each statement was typed on a card and the respondents were handed randomly ordered stacks of cards. . . . They were asked to read through the stack of cards and then to sort them into piles, so that items in the same pile were more similar to each other than items in the other piles. The interviewer did not define the meaning of similarity and respondents used their own definitions [Romney et al., 1979: 307].

How to Do It

To use the pile sort procedure the items to be studied are usually presented on cards. Words or names may be written on index cards (for literates only) or pictures, drawings, or other visual stimuli may be presented (for literates and nonliterates). Cards are shuffled (randomized) before handing them to an informant. Informants are then asked to look through the cards and sort them into piles, so that similar items are in piles together. A subject may be allowed to make as many piles as he or she wants (unconstrained sort) or they may be asked to make a specific number of piles (constrained sort). Pile sort tasks are sometimes constrained to control for individual differences in creating larger, more generic categories ("lumpers") and those who create smaller categories with finer distinctions ("splitters").

If the researcher would like to ask the informants why they have sorted the items as they have, he or she should wait until the informant is finished sorting before asking. Questioning before or during the sorting process might interfere with the categories the informant was going to make and thus bias the results. When the informant is finished, the researcher can ask "In what way are these alike?" or "Why are these together in a pile?" Descriptive answers can be used to interpret final results.

Tabulation

An item-by-item similarity matrix is created from each individual's sort by tabulating the co-occurrence of items in piles so that items that are together are counted as being similar. For example, if we collected data on the similarity of seven items and a respondent put items A, B, and C together in a pile; D and E in a pile; and left F and G by themselves (see Table 3.1) we would create a 7 by 7 table to tabulate similarity among the items. Since A, B, and C are categorized together, A and B are similar, B and C are similar, and A and C are similar. Since D and E are also put together in a pile, D and E are considered to be similar. Thus each pair would get "a point of similarity." This is indicated in the table with a one. For this individual, all other pairs are "dissimilar" and are recorded as zeros. Similarity matrices are tabulated for each individual and then combined across people. The similarity matrix can then be analyzed with a descriptive method such as hierarchical clustering or multidimensional scaling.

Variations

Lumper versus splitter differences in sorting patterns are sometimes counteracted with a constrained pile sort. Here subjects are told how many or how few piles they should make. For example, in the success and failure study, respondents in one sample were asked to sort characteristics into 7 to 9 piles. The results, however, were the same as when informants were allowed to make as many piles as they wanted. Burton (1975) presented a standardization procedure for unconstrained pile sorts that makes adjustments for the different number of piles among informants as well as for different numbers of concepts in each pile. In his normalization procedure, subjects that make a lot of little

TABLE 3.1
Pile Sort Tabulation

An individual's items sorted into piles

Pile 1	Pile 2	Pile 3	Pile 4
A			
B	D		
C	E	F	G

Since A, B, C were together in a pile:

cell (A, B) = 1
cell (A, C) = 1
cell (B, C) = 1

Similarity Matrix

	A	B	C	D	E	F
B	1					
C	1	1				
D	0	0	0			
E	0	0	0	1		
F	0	0	0	0	0	
G	0	0	0	0	0	0

piles (splitters) are weighted more than those who make few, large piles (lumpers). Burton demonstrated the procedure on two separate domains, occupations and behaviors. In both studies, the unconstrained, unnormalized pile sort data performed quite well.

Other variations on the pile sort include "splitting items" so items can be in more than one pile, collecting successive sorts from a single individual, and creating "piles" by selecting items that are most similar to a target item. Stefflre et al. (1971: 86) asked respondents if they thought any items should go in more than one group. If the respondent thought that an item should go into two groups, then the item was "split," an additional card was created for that item, and it was put in both piles. (Tabulation of the similarity data with split items is the same as without split items; with the exception that the split item is similar to items in each pile.) For additional information, Stefflre et al. also asked if any other items should go in a pile; if any things go between piles; to put similar piles together; and to divide that pile into subpiles. These last two questions correspond to successive sorting tasks, where informants are asked to continue grouping items until all items are grouped together in one pile; or where informants are asked to continue subdividing piles until each item is by itself. Successive sorts are one way to elicit a taxonomy from an individual (see Chapter 4 for a discussion of successive sorting procedures).

Since the pile sort is commonly used to study categorizations and dimensions used by informants to categorize stimuli, Rosenberg and Kim (1975) compared the dimensions subjects used in "single sort" and "multiple sort" tasks. In a single sort, informants were given one opportunity to sort items, for example, standard pile sort method. In the multiple sort condition, informants were given multiple opportunities to sort and re-sort items, *each time using a different criterion.* Results indicated that when informants were allowed a single sort, they usually ignored the most obvious dimension of meaning.

The study by Rosenberg and Kim brings up an important point, which may or may not be considered a limitation of the pile sort task. By its nature, the pile sort task cannot accommodate many dimensions of discrimination at once. "Splitters" may try to use multiple dimensions at once, thus resulting in many small piles.

Another modification of the pile sort task is *anchor-point clustering* (Green and Carmone, 1970: 56). With this procedure, informants are asked to consider one item at a time and to select other items that are most like it in meaning. White (1978) used this procedure to collect similarity data among 37 personality descriptors. Data were collected by selecting a target item, shuffling the remaining cards, and asking informants to select five items that were most similar in meaning to the target item. When five items had been matched to a given target item, another target item was selected for consideration, the remaining items were reshuffled and five new items selected. Responses are tabulated into the rows of an N by N table, so that 1's appear under the column items selected as most similar to the row items. Because anchor-point sorting can result in asymmetric similarity data, the table is then "folded onto itself" and corresponding entries from the upper right half are summed with entries from the lower left half. For example, if the similarity between row 1 and column 2 is 1 (sim (A, B) = 1) and the similarity between row 2 and column 1 is also 1 (sim (B, A) = 1), then the similarity between row 2 and column 1 is 2; if sim (A, C) = 0 and sim (C, A) = 1, then sim (C, A) = 1. By summing corresponding entries, asymmetries from data collection are removed.

The pile sort is sometimes called a *Q-sort,* but the more common usage of Q-sort is a variation of a rating scale (see Chapter 6 on Rating Scales; Variations). In the Q-sort, items are rated on a single attribute and informants are instructed to make a specific number of piles usually with a specific number of items in each pile.

Strengths and Weaknesses

The outstanding strength of the pile sort task is the fact that it can accommodate a large number of items. We know of no other data collection method that will allow the collection of judged similarity data among over 100 items. This makes it the method of choice when large numbers are necessary. Other methods that might be used to collect similarity data, such as the triads and paired comparison ratings, become impractical with a large number of items. Depending upon the field conditions under which the researcher is working, he or she may consider using the pile sort for two dozen or more items. There is no hard and fast rule about how many items are too many; with less than 20 items a triad design is preferable (see Chapters 5 and 8 on Triads and Balanced Incomplete Block Design), between 20 to 30 items either can be used, and with more than two dozen items the pile sort is easier to administer.

The pile sort is easy to administer. Informants do not mind sorting things into piles and talking about them. It usually implies a face-to-face interview, although the study by Rosenberg and Kim is an exception. The pile sort can offer other advantages, for example, when real stimuli are being used you need only one of each item to use the pile sort in a field setting. A distinct disadvantage is that unless the items are pictures or actual stimuli, the pile sort cannot be used with nonliterates.

Pile sort data also tend to be "sparse," requiring more informants (say, 20 or more) to obtain stable results. Pile sort data are coded as 0's and 1's; items that appear together in a pile are coded as 1's and items not together are 0's. With some other methods, such as the triads method, a wider range of values is possible resulting in "more data" per person. The more data that are collected per person, the fewer informants are necessary to obtain stable results. Therefore, if you intend to use small sample sizes (say 10 people), we recommend a complete triads design, a balanced incomplete block design with lambda greater than two, or a successive sorting task (see Chapter 4 on Successive Sorts).

A careful reading of the literature indicates that the results of pile sort data collection methods, using medium-size samples between 30 and 40, generally reach reliabilities above .90. The Romney et al. (1979) study demonstrated a high degree of stability across four replications.

Although pile sort data are appropriate for the study of relations among items, it has limited use for the comparison of informants. In a series of articles, Boorman and Arabie (1972), Arabie and Boorman (1973), and Boorman and Olivier (1973) tackled the problem of deriving a metric for the comparison of individuals based on their sorts. Their basic finding is that the difference between "lumpers" (informants who place all items in a few piles) and "splitters" (informants who use a great number of piles with few items in each pile) is so great that it overwhelms all other differences among pile sorts. This implies that, unless one's interest is limited to "lumpers" and "splitters," the pile sort technique is not suitable for the comparison of individuals. However, with an equal number of piles per informant, as is true with a constrained sorting task, comparisons of individuals can be made (see Truex, 1977).

4. PILE SORT II: SUCCESSIVE SORTS AND THE CONSTRUCTION OF TAXONOMIES AND TREES

In this chapter we discuss an extension of the pile sort, that of successively partitioning objects to obtain a taxonomy. Taxonomic or tree-like structures can be obtained in an interview by having informants sort items into groups and splitting those groups into smaller groups or by starting with small groups and merging them into larger and larger groups. These two approaches represent top-down and bottom-up *successive* sorting procedures. Graph theoretic approaches can be used to draw a kind of "tree" using a bottom-up drawing procedure connecting items together. Although the graph construction method is in some ways similar to a bottom-up sort it does not result in a taxonomic structure.

Examples

Tree sorts have been used to study many different topics in a variety of settings. Truex (1977) studied intersubject variations in categorizations of 13 Spanish verbs meaning "to have," for example, had, kept, took. Data were collected from 24 literate males in Oaxaca, Mexico. For the "first cut," informants were asked to sort the verbs into two piles, so that the items within a pile would be similar; there could be any number of items in a pile, but there could be only two piles. On the second cut, each of the initial piles was split into two piles. This sorting/splitting procedure was continued until each subgroup contained one or two items.

Boster (1986) used a top-down sort to study classification of eight color terms. Colors were sorted by two groups of informants. One group did the task verbally (with color names) and the other group did the task nonverbally (with Munsell color chips). Informants were asked to first sort the colors into two piles on the basis of their similarity. The initial split was recorded and subjects were asked to continue subdividing each pile until all the items were separated.

Perchonock and Werner (1968) used a kind of top-down sort to collect a Navaho taxonomy of food. Beginning with a large list of foods eaten by the Navaho, Perchonock and Werner proceeded differently than did Truex and Boster. They began with an unconstrained pile sorting task and then asked their informant to subdivide piles. Using a literate informant, they asked him to begin by sorting the names into piles "using whatever principle" he wanted. They next asked him to name each pile. After the informant provided labels for each of the subsets, the informant was asked to subdivide each, until the smallest subdivision had been reached. Perchonock and Werner report that "several hundred different food names could be completed in a single afternoon" (p. 230). They also constructed a tree drawing of the sorting results and showed it to the informant in order to request further clarification of classification principles.

Freeman et al. (1986) used a bottom-up sort to collect data on social groupings in an ethnographic study of windsurfers. Because they began with the names of many people (54 windsurfers), they began by having informants first sort names into two piles: those they knew and those they did not know. Then, informants were asked to consider only close, intimate, and strong relationships; people that they would always expect to be together—and to create little groupings of people. Next, they were instructed to combine piles, without taking the previous piles apart, and create bigger groups of people. Small piles were successively merged until all people were in one group together or until the informant stopped (typically, when people were divided into two large groups).

How to Do It

As in all data collection techniques, the first step in using the successive sorting procedure is to define the list of items. Though free listing is usually recommended, the domain is sometimes taken from a previous study (as did Boster) or by using an extensive list (as did Perchonock and Werner). You must of course consider whether your informants can read. The successive sorting procedure has been used primarily with literates, although the method can be used with nonliterates if you use visual stimuli such as stuffed birds or color chips. Whether to begin with a top-down or bottom-up approach may be a matter of preference or of what makes most sense given your sorting question. Here we describe the top-down sort.

First, names of items are written on cards or slips of paper. Or, if visual stimuli are to be used they should be assembled. Next, the cards or visual stimuli should be shuffled so that they will be in a random order when presented to informants. For the first cut, the informant is asked to look through or read the items carefully and divide the items into two groups, so that items within each pile are more similar to each other than they are to items in the other pile. For the second cut, the informant is asked to subdivide each of those piles into two piles, creating four piles. This subdivision is continued until each pile contains one or two items.

Tabulation

Top-down sorts, where informants systematically split each pile into two, allow you to (1) create a taxonomic tree for each individual, (2) create an aggregate or group taxonomy, and (3) make interindividual comparisons in structures. Data are recorded at each split or cut. For example, if an informant sorted six items, A, B, C, D, E, F, into two piles, A B and C D E F, record the items in each subgroup. Data, as it is recorded at each step, appear in Table 4.1 The tree that develops is also shown in Table 4.1

Similarity tables also can be created for each step by recording the data into multiple N by N tables. For the first cut, put 1's between all pairs of items that are contained together in a pile. For six items, you need a six by six table to record the similarity among the items. For the informant's two piles, A B and C D E F, record in the lower half of the table a 1 between pair AB for the first pile and 1's for the pairs CD, CE, CF, DE, DF, and EF from the second pile. (Refer to Table 4.2, first cut.) If, for the second cut, our informant split each of the initial two piles into A B C and D E F, we now record the sorting results in a new table. Ones are recorded only for pairs DE, DF, and EF (Table 4.2, cut two). Because many of the items are now singletons, they are "ignored" while the informant continues to split existing piles, so that, on the third cut, our informant may split D E F into D and E F. On the fourth and final cut, E and F would be separated.

Trees can be created for each individual, as in Table 4.1. Group trees, representing several informants' perceptions of the items, can be created by summing together the respondents' data *for a given cut,* for example, summing together one N X N similarity table for each individual. This is equivalent to collecting and analyzing data from a *constrained* pile sort (see previous chapter). The group data can then be represented in tree form with a hierarchical clustering program. Differences between

TABLE 4.1
Resulting Trees

First cut	(AB)		(CDEF)			
Second cut	(A)	(B)	(C)	(DEF)		
Third cut	(A)	(B)	(C)	(D)	(EF)	
Fourth cut	(A)	(B)	(C)	(D)	(E)	(F)

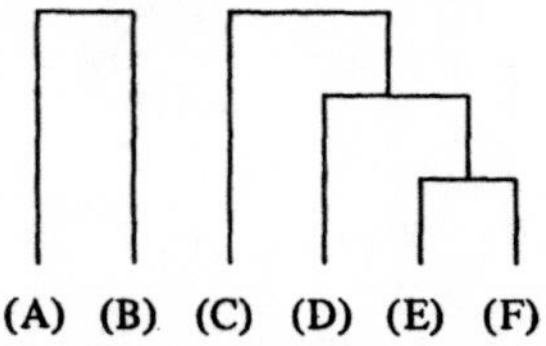

(A) (B) (C) (D) (E) (F)

individuals can be studied by comparing the N X N similarity tables, at the same "cut" or "level."

It is important to remember that for *any given cut,* data can be aggregated across informants, but that the summed matrix for an individual is not a proper similarity matrix and should not be combined with other individuals. Data can be aggregated across subjects for a given cut because the data are synonymous with a constrained pile sort with n piles and each individual's table of data would consist of zeros and ones. For a given cut or set of n piles, the data in the tabulation matrix are meaningful; ones indicate items were in a pile together and zeros mean they were in different piles. The summed cuts for each individual should be aggregated with caution across individuals, because the numbers indicate when a split in the taxonomy was made by a subject and not necessarily how similar two items are. The data reflect the relative similarity among items *within a cluster* and not necessarily the relative similarity between items in different clusters.

In the example presented above, EF are considered to be more similar to each other than either is to D (see Table 4.1). Similarly, DEF are more similar to each other than they are to C. However, it is not clear if the similarity between AB is the same as that between C and DEF or if AB are as similar as EF. In the diagram in Table 4.1, it appears as if AB are not as similar as EF, but height in the tree indicates only when those items were split and not necessarily the level of similarity among those items. D'Andrade (1978) referred to this as a "bare" tree, when you can rank heights or similarity among items only within a cluster. Thus the summed cuts for an individual are helpful if you wish to draw a tree for that individual, but the numbers are not similarity numbers that always make sense if added together with another individual.

Variations

Fillenbaum and Rappoport (1971) used a different kind of bottom-up tree-building procedure. Although their procedure results in a kind

TABLE 4.2
Recording Successive Sorts

First Cut

	A	B	C	D	E	F
A						
B	1					
C	0	0				
D	0	0	1			
E	0	0	1	1		
F	0	0	1	1	1	

Second Cut

	A	B	C	D	E	F
A						
B	0					
C	0	0				
D	0	0	0			
E	0	0	0	1		
F	0	0	0	1	1	

Third Cut

	A	B	C	D	E	F
A						
B	0					
C	0	0				
D	0	0	0			
E	0	0	0	0		
F	0	0	0	0	1	

Summed Cuts

	A	B	C	D	E	F
A						
B	1					
C	0	0				
D	0	0	1			
E	0	0	1	2		
F	0	0	1	2	3	

of "tree" it is actually a connected graph and not a taxonomy. Fillenbaum and Rappoport collected similarity data among items by having informants actually draw "trees." They studied the domains of color names, kinship terms, pronouns, emotion terms, prepositions, conjunctions, verbs meaning to have, verbs of judging, and good-bad terms. Informants were asked to read over a list of items, pick two words that were most similar, write them on paper, and connect them with a line labeled with a 1. Then, they were asked to pick the next most similar pair of words (which could include one already used) and add it to the work sheet and label the line with a 2. Informants were to continue either joining new words to existing words, beginning new links or "subtrees," or joining subtrees together. Each newly added link was numbered (from 1 to N–1) indicating the step at which it was written. This process continued until all the words were connected.

This procedure automatically results in a connected, undirected graph or "tree" but does not force the data into a taxonomic structure. In fact, where Boster's successive sorting of color terms produced a hierarchic structure for each individual, Fillenbaum and Rappoport's procedure could have obtained a ring, with red most similar to orange, orange to yellow, yellow to green, green to blue, blue to violet, and violet to red. The graph theoretic approach to drawing trees allows you to draw a "tree" for each individual; the tree is like the kind of tree that can be drawn with Johnson's hierarchical clustering for connectedness or single-link clustering (Johnson, 1967; Weller and Buchholtz, 1986; also called a minimum spanning tree by Sneath and Sokal, 1973). In addition, because the data are a kind of proximity data, data can be aggregated across informants and group hierarchical trees can be obtained with hierarchical clustering or spatial, dimensional representations can be obtained with multidimensional scaling. Distance data can be estimated between all pairs of items by summing the "length" of the link between items. If A and B are linked together at step one and B and C are linked together at step five, then the distance between A and C is six, the sum of all intermediate links.

Strengths and Weaknesses

Successive sorting tasks are appropriate when it can be assumed that a taxonomic structure is a reasonable representation. A taxonomic structure is an organizing structure, such as an outline. It assumes sets and subsets; headings and subheadings. Further, the "dimensions" that differentiate subgroups in one cluster are different from those in different clusters. Not all domains have underlying taxonomic structures. For example, kinship terms have cross-cutting, discrete features, such as generation, gender, and nuclear versus collateral, and are not best represented in a taxonomy (Romney and D'Andrade, 1964). Domains with "genetic" relations among members, for example, plants and animals, can usually be represented with taxonomies.

Successive sorts provide enough information at the individual level to create a taxonomy for a single individual. A disadvantage of the successive sorting method is that items and domains are forced into taxonomic structures, whether or not such a structure may be appropriate. In general, the sorting task cannot be used orally or with nonliterates.

5. TRIADIC COMPARISONS

The triad method consists of presenting items or objects in sets of three to informants. Triadic comparisons can be used to collect either similarity or ordered data. For similarity data, informants are asked to pick, for each set of three items, the item that is most different from the other two. For ordered data, informants are asked to order the items within each triad from "most" to "least" on some attribute instead of choosing "the most different item." Triadic comparisons can be administered orally.

Examples

Triads have been used extensively in anthropology, psychology, and other fields in the social sciences. One of the early uses was by Romney and D'Andrade (1964) on English kin terms. Many other domains have been studied using the triads methods including: animal terms (Henley, 1969), occupations (Burton, 1968, 1972), disease terms (Lieberman and Dressler, 1977; Weller, 1983; Young and Garro, 1982), and personality descriptors (Romney, Keiffer, and Klein, 1979; Kirk and Burton, 1977; Burton and Kirk, 1979).

Sogn (1979) collected triad similarity data from children dying from leukemia. She interviewed children in a hospital outpatient clinic and collected data on the childrens' perceptions of each other. Children were presented with photographs of clinic children in sets of three and asked to identify two that were most alike in each set. The similarity data were represented spatially with multidimensional scaling. When she presented the results to the children and asked for an interpretation of why Johnny might be similar to Mary, she found that the children were aware of who was sick, who was very sick, and who was dying, even though many of the children had not been told that they were indeed dying.

How to Do It

After establishing the list of study items, triad data may be collected by first enumerating all sets of size three for those items. First, calculate the number of triads that are needed. The number of sets of triads appropriate for a given number of items can be calculated as follows:

$$\begin{matrix} n \\ 3 \end{matrix} = \frac{n!}{3!(n-3!)}.$$

where, n = number of items

so that, with 8 items, there are 56 sets of triads:

$$\begin{matrix} 8 \\ 3 \end{matrix} = \frac{8!}{3!(8-3!)} = \frac{8\cdot7\cdot6\cdot5\cdot4\cdot3\cdot2\cdot1}{3\cdot2\cdot1\cdot5\cdot4\cdot3\cdot2\cdot1} = 56.$$

Then, write-out all possible sets of triads. For 8 items all triadic sets have been enumerated in Table 5.1. Note that this is only practical with small domains, say with 10 or fewer items. The reason is that the number of

TABLE 5.1
Triad Enumeration
(all possible combinations of eight things into sets of size three)

(1)	1	2	3	(20)	1	6	8	(39)	3	4	7
(2)	1	2	4	(21)	1	7	8	(40)	3	4	8
(3)	1	2	5	(22)	2	3	4	(41)	3	5	6
(4)	1	2	6	(23)	2	3	5	(42)	3	5	7
(5)	1	2	7	(24)	2	3	6	(43)	3	5	8
(6)	1	2	8	(25)	2	3	7	(44)	3	6	7
(7)	1	3	4	(26)	2	3	8	(45)	3	6	8
(8)	1	3	5	(27)	2	4	5	(56)	3	7	8
(9)	1	3	6	(28)	2	4	6	(47)	4	5	6
(10)	1	3	7	(29)	2	4	7	(48)	4	5	7
(11)	1	3	8	(30)	2	4	8	(49)	4	5	8
(12)	1	4	5	(31)	2	5	6	(50)	4	6	7
(13)	1	4	6	(32)	2	5	7	(51)	4	6	8
(14)	1	4	7	(33)	2	5	8	(52)	4	7	8
(15)	1	4	8	(34)	2	6	7	(53)	5	6	7
(16)	1	5	6	(35)	2	6	8	(54)	5	6	8
(17)	1	5	7	(36)	2	7	8	(55)	5	7	8
(18)	1	5	8	(37)	3	4	5	(56)	6	7	8
(19)	1	6	7	(38)	3	4	6				

NOTE: Each pair, for example, 1 and 2 or 4 and 6 occurs 6 times.

triads goes up very rapidly with an increase in the number of items. (The total number of triads may be reduced by using a balanced incomplete block triad design. See Chapter 8.)

The next step is to randomize the triads, both by triad order and by position within a triad. Randomization is very important, because triads are usually constructed in a very systematic way and presentation of unrandomized materials can introduce kinds of response bias that would confound results. By numbering the sets from 1 to 56 (for eight items), they can be put into random order with the help of a random number table (Appendix A). To use the random number table pick a spot, say column seven, and move downward using the first two digits, checking for numbers less than or equal to 56 and ignoring numbers that appear more than once. The first number less than or equal to 56 would be the set that should appear first. The first number is 69, so we ignore it. The second number is 27, so the twenty-seventh triad will appear in the first position. The next number is 15, so the fifteenth triad is next. The triad sets are reordered according to those numbers. We used the first four digits in the seventh column and then we used the first four digits of the eighth column. In Table 5.2, the triads have been reordered so that the sets are in random order.

TABLE 5.2
Triads Randomized by Sets and Position

(27)	5	4	2	(22)	3	4	2	(41)	6	3	5
(15)	8	1	4	(50)	6	4	7	(31)	2	5	6
(39)	4	7	3	(52)	8	4	7	(35)	2	8	6
(18)	8	1	5	(30)	2	4	8	(48)	5	4	7
(38)	4	6	3	(14)	4	1	7	(44)	7	6	3
(56)	8	6	7	(21)	7	8	1	(42)	7	5	3
(36)	2	7	8	(16)	1	5	6	(5)	1	2	7
(47)	5	4	6	(1)	1	3	2	(7)	3	1	4
(55)	8	5	7	(12)	5	1	4	(23)	5	3	2
(45)	3	6	8	(51)	8	6	4	(40)	8	3	4
(32)	7	5	2	(17)	7	5	1	(3)	1	5	2
(37)	4	3	5	(10)	3	1	7	(24)	2	3	6
(26)	3	8	2	(13)	1	4	6	(2)	4	2	1
(28)	6	4	2	(43)	5	8	3	(54)	6	8	5
(29)	2	7	4	(33)	2	5	8	(8)	3	1	5
(6)	8	2	1	(34)	7	6	2	(4)	6	2	1
(20)	6	8	1	(25)	2	7	3	(53)	5	7	6
(9)	3	1	6	(46)	8	3	7	(49)	5	8	4
(11)	1	8	3	(19)	6	1	7				

Next, the position of items within each triad is randomized. Since there are only three positions, first, second, and third (1, 2, 3), the original sets need to be randomly reordered into 1, 2, 3; 1, 3, 2; 2, 1, 3; 2, 3, 1; 3, 1, 2; and 3, 2, 1. To randomize the order within a triad, a die could be rolled with each of the six sides symbolizing a particular order. We have appended a list of randomizations for within triad orders (Appendix B). Using the randomized positions from Appendix B, we see the first order should be 3, 2, 1 (6). The second order should be 3, 1, 2 (5) and the third order, 2, 3, 1 (4); and so on. Since the triads are currently all in the order 1, 2, 3, they must be reordered *within* each triad. The items in the first triad, then, are reordered from their present order, 1, 2, 3, to the new order, 2, 1, 3. Thus the first set changes from 2, 4, 5 (in Table 5.1) to 5, 4, 2 (in Table 5.2). The next triad is reordered from 1, 2, 3 to 3, 1, 2. So, the second triad (originally triad 15) is reordered from 1, 4, 8 to 8, 1, 4. The final triad form randomized both by sets and position appears as Table 5.2. To use the solution set, simply substitute the name of each item in place of each number.

With a triad form ready, you are now ready to collect data either orally or with a written questionnaire. The interview should begin with instructions and a few examples. It is important that the examples are from a different domain so as not to influence the answers of your informant[s].

To collect rank order data, informants are asked to rank the items in each set from one to three. In an oral ranking task, read all three items in a set and ask the informant to choose the one that is the "most x." Then, read the remaining two items and ask again, "which is the most x?"

To collect similarity data, informants are instructed to select the item in each set that is most different in meaning from the other two. For example, the following instructions were given to college students on a written questionnaire:

> This is a task concerning the meaning of words. You will be given sets of three words. In each set of words, circle the one which is *most* different in meaning from the others. For example:
> house woman building
> In this example, circle *woman*, since it is most different in meaning from the other two words. Now try the next example,
> man woman grass
> Do all of the problems, even if you are not sure of the answers. DO NOT SKIP ANY sets of words. if you are not sure of the answer, make the best guess you can.

These instructions can be modified according to whom the informants are. While the above instructions work quite well in a classroom with undergraduates, they need to be modified for oral administration. It is important that informants understand and "correctly" answer a couple of examples before beginning the interview.

Although many of the analytical tools for analyzing judged similarity data uncover dimensions that informants use to discriminate among items, researchers sometimes like to add interpretive data by asking informants why they made the choices they did. When similarity data are collected with a pile sort method, a natural time to inquire about why things are similar is *after* the informant has finished grouping things into piles. This is the natural and appropriate time to ask. Similarly with the triads, the appropriate time to ask is after the informant has finished making all his or her choices. Interruptions may introduce unknown kinds of biases in the choices that follow.

The responses about why pairs may or may not be similar can add interesting ethnographic information to the interpretation of results, although it is not necessary to collect. An equally valid and perhaps better technique is to present the results of your analysis to your informants and ask them to explain the results to you. Of course, this is a more expensive technique both in terms of time and energy, but it can provide insightful information.

Tabulation

Triad data are tabulated according to the type of data collected. If informants were asked to rank the items in each triad, the ranks are summed across items to obtain a complete ordering of items for each informant. If informants were asked to judge the similarity of items in each set, then responses are tabulated into a similarity matrix.

With similarity data, the responses of each subject are tallied into a similarity matrix. For eight items, an 8 by 8 table is created and, since this type of similarity data is symmetric, only the lower left half of the square table is used. For example, in Table 5.3 appear a subject's responses to three triads. In the first triad the subject has identified "grandson" as being most different from "son" and "brother." Thus "son" and "brother" are perceived as similar in some way, and are tabulated into that person's similarity matrix; a one is tallied into the cell representing brother, son. When finished, there would be a tally mark for each triad in the similarity matrix. The tally marks are summed, so that the similarity between any pair is the number of tallies they received. It is easiest to do a separate matrix for each individual and then sum all of those matrices into one, aggregate matrix. The aggregate table then would be ready for a descriptive analysis by hierarchical clustering, multidimensional scaling or some other procedure.

Variations

A variation on triad pick-the-most-different-item similarity data is the *full triad* method. Torgerson (1958) and Henley (1969) used the full method of triad collection. Items were presented in sets of three and informants asked (1) to pick the two that were most similar, and (2) to pick the two that were most different. The full method ranks each pair of items in a triad in terms of their similarity. Each triad contains 3 pairs; AB, AC, and BC are contained in the set ABC. If AB are chosen as the most similar and AC as least similar, then the three pairs are ranked as AB (= 3) most similar, BC (= 2) medium, and AC (= 1) least similar. The data are tabulated as described above, except that the ranks are summed into the similarity matrix.

Balanced, incomplete block (BIB) designs are a variation of triads that minimize the number of triads necessary while maintaining a balanced comparison of items. As the number of items increases, so does the number of triads: with 21 items, there would be 1,330 triads. Clearly, that's too many for an average interview! What's needed is a way to eliminate some triads and yet maintain a balanced comparison of all

TABLE 5.3
Triad Tabulation

Brother	Son	Grandson
Cousin	Grandfather	Son
Son	Nephew	Father

Similarity Matrix

	Grandfather	Grandson	Father	Son	Brother	Uncle	Cousin
Grandfather							
Grandson							
Father							
Son	1		1				
Brother				1			
Uncle							
Cousin							
Nephew							

pairs of items. BIB designs work by controlling the number of times each pair is compared. In the complete triad design mentioned above with 8 items, creating 56 triads, each pair actually occurs six times (see Table 5.1). By minimizing the number of times each pair occurs, the overall number of triads can be decreased. If each pair occurred only once, 21 items can be compared in 70 triads instead of the 1,330 triads in the complete design. (Refer to Chapter 8 on Balanced Incomplete Block Designs.)

Strengths and Weaknesses

Triads can be administered either orally or as a paper-and-pencil task. In our experience it is very easy for informants to understand what is desired and the method makes it fairly easy to get very stable results from nonliterate informants. Triads are not practical for comparisons among a large number of items in a domain. Due to the number of triads produced by the complete design it is only feasible to use 8 or 10 items using the complete design. Even with balanced incomplete block designs, the method becomes impractical with more than 25 items.

6. RATING SCALES

Rating scales are one of the more common ways of collecting data in the social sciences. Scales can represent any of a number of concepts. For example, illness terms can be rated on their degree of severity, cars can be rated on "likelihood to purchase" scales, and political candidates can be rated on how well liked their policies are. Items can be rated on a single conceptual scale or each may be rated on a series of scales representing a variety of concepts or attributes. Frequently rating scales are combined to create indices. Although rating scales are usually used to collect ordered data, they may also be used to collect similarity data. To collect similarity data, pairs of items are rated on a scale of similarity. Rating scales are most reliable with literates in a written format.

Examples

Rating scales are the most widely used technique for questionnaire data collection. The popularity of rating scales is probably due to the fact that they are a familiar format to educated North Americans and they can be administered to large numbers of respondents with written questionnaires and survey instruments.

Osgood and colleagues used rating scales to study the dimensions of meaning in words. In the same way that physical objects can be described in terms of their length, width, and height, and colors in terms of their hue, saturation, and brightness, Osgood and colleagues described the dimensions of affective meaning as evaluative (good-bad), active (active-passive), and potency (strong-weak). A diverse set of words were rated on large sets of bipolar adjectives to determine underlying dimensions of meaning. Scales were considered to be similar to the extent that they had similar response patterns across words. Words were considered to be similar in meaning if they were rated similarly across scales. Similarity in meaning, did not indicate the degree to which words were synonymous; instead, they were similar in the sense that they evoked similar "feelings."

Materials were collected for a cross-national study in three phases (Osgood et al., 1975: 22). In the first phase, a "diverse sample of 100 culture-common, translation-equivalent substantives (nouns)" were presented to informants and they were asked to name the first "qualifier (adjective)" that occurred to them. The 10,000 responses that were obtained were analyzed for frequency, diversity, and independence of usage across the 100 nouns and a subset was selected. A small number of informants were then used to generate opposites for the subset of qualifiers. Items without clear opposites were eliminated. A final list of 50 pairs was used to create seven-point scales and to rate the original list of 100 items.

Respondents were instructed to rate a series of items, for example, "MY MOTHER, THE CHINESE, MODERN ART" on a series of "bipolar seven-step scales defined by verbal opposites (e.g., good-bad, strong-weak, fast-slow, fair-unfair)" (Osgood et al., 1975: 41). For example:

MY MOTHER

good ____ : ____ : ____ : ____ : ____ : ____ : ____ bad
weak ____ : ____ : ____ : ____ : ____ : ____ : ____ strong

Informants were instructed to judge the meaning of words on the basis of what the word meant to them (Osgood et al., 1975: 83). Scale steps were defined in terms of how closely related the item at the top of the page was related to one or the other of the ends of the scale. The ends of the scale indicated that the item was *very closely related* (±3); the next step (±2) indicated *quite closely related;* and ±1 indicated *only slightly related.* Note that because this is an odd numbered scale, there is a neutral category. The midpoint can indicate *neutrality, equally associated,* or *completely irrelevant.* Osgood et al. (1975: 41) defined the midpoint as "equally X and Y," "either X or Y," or "neither X nor Y"; emphasizing "equally X and Y" to encourage "metaphorical thinking."

In a methodologic study, Dawes (1977) used five different rating scale formats to estimate the height of his colleagues. Each scale was modified from its original source so that it referred to height. An interesting aspect of the study is that he also had the actual height of each person to validate the results. The first scale had six ordinal categories from -3 "extremely short" to + 3 "extremely tall." Both numbers and adjectives were used on the scale and there was no neutral category. The second example (adapted from the work of Osgood and colleagues) had seven categories and the end points were anchored with adjectives opposite in meaning (tall, short). The third scale was asymmetric with three tall categories and one short category. The fourth was a 100-point scale, marked with numbers every 20 units, and with five labels. The fifth had 25 categories with six labels at equally spaced intervals.

Each respondent rated five people on each scale so that all 25 people were rated by 5 raters on each of the 5 scales. Dawes averaged the responses of each of the five raters for each person, producing a set of 25 values for each scale. He then correlated the averaged ratings with actual height for each person. All of the scales performed quite well. Correlations between rated height and actual height ranged from .88 to .94. The "worst" scales were the third and fourth scales, indicating that simply increasing the number of points in a scale does not necessarily make a scale better.

How to Do It

The first step is to decide on the items to be studied and the scale(s) to be used. The scale "concept" should be derived from the purpose of the study. For example, if you are studying the prestige of various occupations, then it follows that the occupations should be rated on a prestige scale. All items should be rated on the same scale or set of scales. Scale anchors should be expressed in terms of the concept scale, for example, extremely prestigious, prestigious, and slightly prestigious. Scales are usually expressed as four- to eleven-point scales, unless administered orally. For oral administration, two- to four-point scales can be used (see section below on variations).

Similarity data can be collected with rating scales if informants rate pairs of items on a scale of similarity. First, all possible pairs of items become the "items" being rated. Then, each pair is rated on a scale of "similarity."

After deciding upon items and scales, a questionnaire is prepared. Rating scales work best with literate informants in a written format. Rating scales are probably best presented next to each item. If items in a single domain are to be rated on multiple concepts, all items should be rated on a single concept before proceeding onto the next concept. Alternatively, an item may be rated on all concepts before proceeding onto the next item. The former presentation should be adhered to when study items are from a single domain and they are rated on a few specific concepts. Researchers should be warned that when items are rated on more than one concept there is a real danger of the rating scales interfering with one another. The latter method seems to be appropriate in the case where the study items do not make up a single domain or if many semantic differentials are to be used. It is in the latter case where the analysis tends to focus somewhat more on the adjectives.

Rating scales can be presented numerically or graphically. Scale steps and end points are referred to as "anchors." Scale anchor points help respondents use the scales with similar definitions in mind. Some scales are anchored linguistically, usually with adjectives and modifying adverbs. Cliff (1959) studied the effect that particular quantifiers have on decreasing or increasing the intensity of an adjective. For example, the modifier "slightly" decreases the intensity of an adjective by half, while "extremely" increases the intensity by 50%. Thus slightly pleasant, pleasant, and extremely pleasant, create similar increments in intensity. Scales can be anchored with positive and negative degrees of the same concept or with bipolar adjectives (hot to cold, or hard to soft). Scales anchored with bipolar opposites are usually referred to as semantic differentials. Numbers can also be used to anchor rating scales, either alone or in conjunction with labels. Some less common ways of anchoring scales include actual examples of the quality being rated or the use of pictures, for example, different degrees of "happy faces" to show agreement.

Many discussions have focused on how many scale steps to use and whether or not there should be an odd or even number of steps. A scale can vary from a two-point to a hundred-point scale. A two-point scale is simply a dichotomous response agree/disagree, true/false (see the chapter on other formats, section on dichotomous format). The popular belief is that more scale steps are better than few. Item reliability increases as the number of steps increases from 2 to 20, but reliability begins to stabilize at around 7 to 11 steps (Guilford, 1954; Nunnally, 1978: 595). There is no magic number of steps and the choice of seven-point scales by many researchers is probably due as much to custom as any other reason; seven is not the number of choice because of human memory and processing limitations as some have suggested.

The choice of an odd or even number of steps affects whether or not there will be a middle, neutral category. Some researchers prefer an odd number of steps so that if the scale does not apply or if both ends of the scale apply equally (as with the semantic differential) respondents may choose the neutral category. On the other hand, some respondents may "overuse" the middle category. An even number of categories forces respondents to choose one way or the other. An advantage of even numbered scales is that if the data are recategorized and collapsed into two categories (as often happens) there are no equivocal responses. Whether to use an odd or an even number of steps is left up to the researcher.

A more important issue in the use of rating scales is whether or not each respondent uses all of the steps. Rating scales are extremely sensitive to response bias, the propensity of an individual to use one end of the scale or a narrow range in the middle of the scale. If a number of items have been rated on a rating scale, the frequency of responses for each step should form an approximately normal distribution. The theory is that since many things in the world are normally distributed, the distribution of judgments should reflect that distribution. The Q-sort is a variation of the rating scale that controls the shape of the distribution in responses (see section below on variations).

Tabulation

Data can be analyzed for each respondent or in aggregate form for all respondents. At the individual level, 21 occupations rated on a seven-point prestige scale would order the occupations into seven ordinal categories (provided the informant used all seven categories). At a group level, responses can be averaged across informants. However, problems with response bias usually dictate that data be standardized within individuals prior to averaging. When similarity data are collected with rating scales, the similarity between pairs of items is recorded in the appropriate cells in a similarity matrix and summed across informants.

Variations

Rating scales do not readily lend themselves to oral interviewing. The possible exceptions are two-point, three-point, and four-point scales. The two-point scale is actually a dichotomous choice question, where the requested response is true/false, yes/no, agree/disagree, buy/not buy, and so on (see Chapter 10 on dichotomous format). Because of response bias problems (sometimes informants have a tendency to repeat the first choice, the last choice, or simply to agree with everything), each question can be asked twice. For example (Weller, 1983), instead of asking "Does ____ need hot or cold remedies in order to get cured?" asked, "Does ____ need *cold* remedies in order to get cured?" and again later in the interview, "Does ____ need *hot* remedies in order to get cured?"

Oral rating scales tend not to yield stable responses, as response bias is exacerbated. Anchor points can change in meaning between individuals and between items. Rating scales seem to require a more complex concept of ordination, whereas pair comparisons do not (see Chapter 7 on ranking). It is our opinion that comparative ranking procedures provide more reliable and valid data than do rating scales.

While some work in the United States by survey researchers using telephone interviews have experimented with rating scales, the most innovative use is the four-point scale that is asked in a series of two questions (Frey, 1983: 121-124). If the scale ranges from 1 = strongly disagree, 2 = somewhat disagree, 3 = somewhat agree, and 4 = strongly agree, the first question is whether or not the respondent agrees with some statement; "Some people think ____. Do you agree or disagree with this statement?" Depending upon the answer given, the next question is "Do you agree (disagree) strongly or only somewhat?" The first question places the response into either the 1, 2 or 3, 4 categories. The second question locates the response as either a 1, 2, 3, or 4.

A variation of the rating scale that can be done in a face-to-face interview is the Q-sort. With the Q-sort, respondents are asked to rate items by sorting the items into a specified number of piles (Nunnally, 1978: 613-616). The "rating scale" is usually indicated on a table top, for example, with seven index cards labeled from 1 = "prefer the least" to 7 = "prefer the most." With the items to be rated also written on cards, respondents are asked to sort them into seven piles, from those items that they prefer the most to those items they prefer the least. The sorting task is usually further constrained, although it need not be, so that a specified number of items must go in each pile to make the distribution approximately normal.

Strengths and Weaknesses

One of the main advantages of the rating scale is the ease of administration and its familiarity. It does, however, require literate informants or visual stimuli. Rating scales can have severe problems. Anchor points are not necessarily comparable between and within subjects. Response effects, preferences for the first, middle, or last position on the scale, may make it difficult to compare data between respondents. Rating scales do not lend themselves to oral interviewing, as response bias effects are exacerbated (primacy and recency effects). The Q-sort (controlling the number of items in each pile) is an exception. The Q-sort is not sensitive to response bias and can be used in a face-to-face interview. Rating scales are not necessarily improved by increasing the width or number of points in the scale or by adding an apparent metric. Also, the "meaningfulness" of rating scales in general is questionable (Roberts, 1985).

7. RANK ORDER METHODS: COMPLETE AND PARTIAL TECHNIQUES

Rank order methods require informants to rank items in terms of a specific characteristic, for example, occupations in terms of prestige, soft drinks in terms of preference, or animals in terms of size. The *complete rank ordering* methods usually require that informants be literate. *Partial rank order* methods present informants with only a small subset of items at a time and a complete rank order can be inferred. In cases where the subsets consist of just two items the task reduces to judging which item has "most" of the characteristics under consideration and is called the method of "paired comparisons." In this chapter we present a number of ways of collecting rank order data, including many that are appropriate for nonliterate informants.

Full Rank Order Data Collection

Rank order data can be collected in a variety of ways. The most straightforward way is to simply have all n items ranked from 1 to n. Literate respondents can be presented with a written form, with the items in random order, and asked to order the items from "most" to "least" by putting numbers next to each item, so that 1 = the most, 2, 3 . . . and n = the least. For example, Romney et al. (1986) had undergraduates order 34 possible causes of death from most to least frequent using such a pencil-and-paper task.

Another way to collect full ranked data, although more time consuming, is to present each informant with a stack of cards containing written or visual stimuli and ask them to order the cards from "most" to "least" or from "best" to "worst," and so on. It is extremely important that the cards be shuffled once or twice between informants (to randomize them), so that each informant does not see the order produced by the previous person.

Weller (1980: 35-36) used a card sorting task to have women rank order disease terms on different concepts. Because she had approximately 30 items, data were collected by first asking the women to read through the cards/diseases and to sort them into two piles, that is, to put the most contagious diseases into one pile and the least contagious diseases into another pile. Then, with one pile set aside, the most contagious disease terms were spread out and the items were ranked by having informants remove cards, one at a time, from the array. Informants were asked to pick the most contagious disease and that card was removed and set aside. This was repeated until all items were ordered, in single-file, next to the original array. The final order was checked by asking, for adjacent pairs of items, "Is ______ more contagious than ______?" allowing informants to make modifications if they wished. The entire process was repeated for the pile of items judged to be less contagious and the two orders were combined, creating a complete ordering of disease terms on contagion.

Although the card sort can be used with literates or non-literates to order visual stimuli or actual items (e.g., fruits or stuffed birds), it cannot be used to rank abstract concepts when working with non-literates. Rank ordering tasks can be broken down into simpler paired comparisons so that items can be ordered orally. The task can be simplified by using a paired comparison, balanced incomplete block design, or a sorting method such as the quicksort to collect the order. The balanced incomplete block designs, quicksort, and merge sort shorten a ranking task by minimizing the number of paired comparisons that are necessary to obtain a complete rank order. Since some of these variations are rather complicated, we devote a special section to each of them.

Partial Methods: Paired Comparisons

In a paired comparison task, items are presented two at a time and respondents are asked which is "more" or which is "less." For n items, a pair comparison design creates $n(n - 1)/2$ pairs. For example, if we wanted someone to order ten items using this method, we would create the 45 pairs and randomize the order both within and between pairs (randomization is discussed in Chapter 5 on Triads). For each pair, informants are asked which is "more." A total order is obtained by summing the number of times each item was chosen. Note that large numbers indicate the response to your question; in this case, large numbers indicate "more" and small numbers indicate "less."

In a study of disease concepts in rural Mexico, informants orally rank ordered ten diseases on four different concepts (Weller, 1984b). Using a complete paired comparison design, all 45 pairs were read to the informants. For each pair, the informant was asked which was "more," for example, "Which is more contagious, ______ or ______ ?" A complete rank order was created for each person by counting the number of times each item was identified as being "more contagious."

Paired comparisons may be collected orally or in a written format. When interviewing is done orally, each pair is read and the respondent is asked to choose one. In a written format, informants are asked to mark the item that is "more" either by checking or circling one item in each pair or by ranking the items within each pair so that 2 = more and 1 = less. Unless items have been ranked, items identified as "more" are coded as 1's. Items in each pair that are "less" are coded with 0's. Items may be coded with either 1, 2 (as in the ranked case) or 0, 1 values.

A complete ordering is obtained for each informant by summing the responses for each item. Essentially, the rank of an item is a sum of the number of times it was chosen. To tabulate the responses, simply sum together all the codes or ranks assigned to each item. If 0, 1 codes are used one can be added to each of the final ranks so that items are ordered from 1 to n instead of 0 to n - 1. Also in this tabulation, large numbers indicate "more" and small numbers "less."

One advantage of paired comparisons besides the ease with which they can be administered orally is that responses can be analyzed for consistency. A consistent answer occurs when a person says A is greater than B, B is greater than C, and A is greater than C. Inconsistent answers contain a logical contradiction: elephant is larger than goat, goat is larger than mouse, and mouse is larger than elephant. When a pair from any set of three pairs does not permit three items to be in perfect order, the responses contain inconsistencies.

Inconsistent answers occur for a variety of reasons. First, respondents can make errors. Some errors are unintentional, others are not. Large numbers of inconsistent answers can indicate that your respondent is "pulling your leg." She or he may not want to answer the questions, or for some other reason is answering nonsense. Second, if an informant cannot tell the difference between two items, for example, they may consider A and B to be the same size, and so on, answers comparing A or B to other items may be idiosyncratic. Finally, the less salient the question is to the informant, the more errors you would expect the informant to make. In the study of disease concepts in rural Mexico mentioned above, when informants were asked to order disease terms on a highly salient dimension of illness—severity—informants made few inconsistent answers. When asked whether a disease needed hot or cold remedies in order to get cured, the error rate went up. Unfortunately, all three reasons can be confounded together. Guilliksen and Tucker (1961) provide a test to test if informants' answers are significantly different from random.

A disadvantage of paired comparisons is that the number of pairs necessary to compare a set of items goes up rapidly as the number of items increases. With 10 items, 45 pairs are necessary. With 15 items, 105 pairs are necessary.

Triads and Balanced Incomplete Block Designs

Since the number of pairs goes up rapidly as the number of items increases, a full paired comparison ranking task can become unwieldy. Balanced incomplete block designs and triads minimize the number of actual pair comparisons that need to be made to obtain a complete rank order. Balanced incomplete block designs simplify the ordering task by reducing the number of paired comparisons that are necessary by presenting items in subsets larger than two. Paired comparisons may be thought of as ranking each pair of objects on some variable. It is possible to take triples, quadruples, and so on in the same way. Thus items may be arranged in subsets of three each (triads) and informants asked to order each set of items from most to least. As with the paired comparison design, a complete rank order is obtained by summing the ranks assigned to each item. These designs are easy to use in either oral or written interviews and allow for the calculation of the internal consistency within an individual's responses (Guilliksen and Tucker, 1961). Although a complete paired comparison of 13 items would take 78 pairs, 13 items can be compared in 26 sets with 3 items per set or in 13 sets with 4 items when a balanced, incomplete block design is used. (Refer to Chapters 5 and 8 on Triads and Balanced Incomplete Block Designs.)

Quicksort and Merge Sort

Another way to collect ordered data from informants orally is with a sorting technique, the quicksort. Quicksort is similar to the card sort used by Weller (1980) except that it does not require that informants know how to read. This method is easy to use with both literates and nonliterates. Quicksort and the merge sort are ordering techniques developed in computer science (Knuth, 1973). Both minimize the number of paired comparisons by assuming transitivity. In other words, if an informant has judged A to be greater than B and B greater than C, then you assume that A is greater than C and you do not ask about that pair. Quicksort, on the average, will require fewer paired comparisons than the merge sort and in the worst case they both will be equivalent to asking about all possible pairs of items. In the following illustration we show how the quicksort can order eight items with only 14 paired comparisons, instead of using all possible comparisons of 28 pairs.

With the *quicksort*, cards are first shuffled (randomized) and a card (the first, the last, or any card) is selected as a "standard." All cards are compared to the standard and are divided into two piles: the cards "greater than" the standard and those "less than" the standard. This process is repeated for each pile, until all items are ordered. If we begin with eight items:

E, B, F, D, C, G, H, A

and select the first item, E, as the standard, we begin by comparing each of the seven remaining items with E, asking is B more than E? Is F more than E? If an item is more than E, it goes into the "more than" pile, otherwise it goes into the "less than" pile. In this example, we would get:

(B D C A) E (F G H)

on the first pass. We would then select an item in the first pile, say B, and compare all other items in that pile to it, so D, C, and A would be compared to B, splitting the subpile into two new piles:

(A) B (D C) E (F G H).

Since A is in a pile by itself it does not need to be compared to anything. D and C are compared to each other, resulting in a complete ordering of the first subpile:

A, B, C, D, E (F G H)

We now repeat the process with the second subpile. F is selected as the standard and G and H are compared to it:

A, B, C, D, E, F (G H).

Since G and H form a pile by themselves, they are then compared to each other. With final comparison of G and H, the entire list is ordered:

A, B, C, D, E, F, G, H.

Nerlove and Walters (1977) provide an example of the use of a *merge sort*. They used pictures of children with nonliterate mothers to obtain rankings of "smartness" among the children. Because many of the adults did not know all of the children and because they were not able to anticipate which children an adult would or would not know, they chose not to use a balanced incomplete block design. Instead, they used the merge sort technique to minimize the number of comparisons, limiting the number of pairs that are needed by assuming transitivity.

To use the merge sort to order items in terms of some quality, the names or pictures are first arranged into pairs. Items in each pair are ordered, creating ordered sublists. Lists are merged by comparing the first or top item from one list with the item at the top of another list. This process is continued until there are no more items left in each sublist, creating new, longer ordered lists. As with the quicksort, the final ordering can be reviewed by asking the informant about adjacent pairs.

Strengths and Weaknesses

The complete ranking is a very powerful data collection technique and has several strengths. First, it contains a great deal of information and is productive for the time spent by the informant. If we had good measures of how much information could be obtained per minute of informant time for each of the methods presented in this book, we would expect that the ranking method would be the best producer. The method is ideal for the study of individual differences. Precise measures are possible of how similar each informant is to each other informant. However, there are some kinds of questions that do not lend themselves to ranking. Questions of judged similarity are not appropriate for ranking in general although there are exceptions. Ordering methods can become somewhat tedious for nonliterates.

Paired comparisons are probably the easiest and most reliable method to use with illiterates when there are a dozen or fewer items to be ordered. Quicksort is an easy and efficient way to order a large list of items, especially when working with illiterates. Quicksort is probably more interesting than a full paired comparison or balanced incomplete block design to do, although it can take as much time and consistency cannot be measured. One criticism of quicksort is that if an error is made in the initial or any subsequent split, it cannot be corrected. This may be compensated for by making a quick review of the order, asking about adjacent pairs. Items not in order are allowed to float down or up to their correct position (a modified Bubblesort).

8. BALANCED-INCOMPLETE BLOCK DESIGNS

In this chapter we describe how data collection tasks involving comparisons of subsets of items can be shortened with the use of *balanced incomplete block designs* (BIBs). One advantage of BIB designs is that larger numbers of items can be studied than with complete designs. Ordination (rank order) or similarity (triad comparison) tasks can be simplified and collected orally. For example, high school students that have difficulty ranking twenty-one disciplinary actions from most to least severe have less difficulty ranking items when they have been arranged into twenty-one sets of five each (items in each set are then ranked from one to five).

Balanced-incomplete block designs systematically compare subsets of items. The designs work by controlling the number of times that *each pair* is compared. By reducing the number of times each pair occurs with or is compared to other items, the total number of subsets is reduced, while still maintaining comparisons among all items. With seven items, a complete triad design, for example, takes 35 sets of size three (Table 8.1). In that design, each pair actually occurs five times. If the number of times each pair occurs is reduced from five to one, comparison data can be obtained among all items, but it only takes seven triads (Table 8.2). Note that all pairs occur, but each pair occurs only once. This basic design can be expanded so that each pair appears twice, in 14 triads, by creating *another* set of seven triads, for example, by reassigning numbers to items and creating seven new triads. Similarly, designs can be created where each pair occurs three times (in 21 triads), four times (in 28 triads), and, finally, the full design of five times (in 35 triads). As it turns out, BIB designs are not always so straightforward, for sometimes solutions simply do not exist. BIB designs are identified with three parameters: n, the number of items; lambda (λ), the number of times each pair occurs; k, the number of items in each set or block; and b, the number of sets or blocks. Table 8.3 indicates where solutions are and are not possible. Note in the table, that although solutions ($k = 3$) are possible for seven items, such is not the case for eight items.

BIB designs can shorten a data collection task by reducing the number of subsets. Subsets of size three are appropriate for similarity data collection (see Chapter 5 on Triads). BIB designs can also be used to shorten and simplify rank order data collection using subset sizes of three or more (see Chapter 7 on Rank Order Methods).

Examples

Kirk and Burton (1977) used a BIB design to collect data on the meaning of personality descriptors among the Maasai. To study possible contextual shifts in meaning of personality traits across age and sex categories, they collected similarity data among 13 personality trait descriptors and varied the social identity term that they modified. A BIB design for 13 items, $\lambda = 2$, with 52 triads was used to collect the similarity data. Eight different sets of similarity data were collected, seven sets corresponded to categories of age-sex social identity modified by the personality descriptors and one set consisted of personality descriptors without reference to person. The 13 personality descriptors were selected from a larger set of 50 terms that were elicited from Maasai informants and from Maasai conversations. Each of the eight triads tests were administered to a separate sample of 30 informants. Items were presented to informants three at a time and for each set, respondents were asked to pick "the one most different in meaning from the other two" (p. 739). Interviews were conducted in the Maasai language by Maasai research assistants. Similarity was tabulated for

TABLE 8.1
Complete Triads Design for Seven Items

(1)	1	2	3	(13)	1	5	6	(25)	2	6	7
(2)	1	2	4	(14)	1	5	7	(26)	3	4	5
(3)	1	2	5	(15)	1	6	7	(27)	3	4	6
(4)	1	2	6	(16)	2	3	3	(28)	3	4	7
(5)	1	2	7	(17)	2	3	5	(29)	3	5	6
(6)	1	3	4	(18)	2	3	6	(30)	3	5	7
(7)	1	3	5	(19)	2	3	7	(31)	3	6	7
(8)	1	3	6	(20)	2	4	5	(32)	4	5	6
(9)	1	3	7	(21)	2	4	6	(33)	4	5	7
(10)	1	4	5	(22)	2	4	7	(34)	4	6	7
(11)	1	4	6	(23)	2	5	6	(35)	5	6	7
(12)	1	4	7	(24)	2	5	7				

TABLE 8.2
Triads Design for Seven Items—Each Pair Appears Once

Triads				*Pairs in each triad*		
(1)	1	2	3	(1, 2)	(1, 3)	(2, 3)
(2)	1	4	5	(1, 4)	(1, 5)	(4, 5)
(3)	1	6	7	(1, 6)	(1, 7)	(6, 7)
(4)	2	4	6	(2, 4)	(2, 6)	(4, 6)
(5)	2	5	7	(2, 5)	(2, 7)	(5, 7)
(6)	3	4	7	(3, 4)	(3, 7)	(4, 7)
(7)	3	5	6	(3, 5)	(3, 6)	(5, 6)

each pair of items: Whenever an item was chosen as "most different" in a triad, the remaining two items were judged to be similar.

When collecting rank order data, especially from young or uneducated persons, you may want to "simplify" the task. Ranking items from 1 to n presumes a moderate amount of education on the part of the informant. The task can be simplified by having informants rank small subsets of items. Paired comparisons are an example of a way to present items in "manageable" subsets; informants are asked, for each pair, which is "more" (or which is "less") and from this information a complete ordering can be obtained (see Chapter 7). Similarly, items can be presented in subsets of three or more at a time and informants asked to order the items in each set.

Weller and Dungy (1986: 541) explored women's preferences for infant feeding methods by having women rank order descriptive statements in terms of their relative desirability.

> Women who could not or did not want to read ranked a subset of the twenty items orally. A balanced, incomplete block design was used to

TABLE 8.3
Some Balanced-Incomplete Block Designs
for Blocks with Seven or Fewer Items

	Number of items, n	*Number of blocks, b*	*Number of pairs, λ*
Block size, k = 3	7	7	1
	9	12	1
	10	30	2
	12	44	2
	13	26	1
	15	35	1
	16	80	2
	19	57	1
	21	70	1
	25	100	1
Block size, k = 4	8	14	3
	9	18	3
	10	15	2
	12	33	3
	13	13	1
	16	20	1
	25	50	1
	28	63	1
Block size, k = 5	11	11	2
	15	21	2
	21	21	1
	25	30	1
Block size, k = 6	16	16	2
	16	24	3
	21	28	2
	31	31	1
Block size, k = 7	15	15	3
	22	22	2
	28	36	2
	43	43	1
	49	56	1

minimize the number of paired comparisons and to obtain a complete rank order scale for 13 items for each woman. Those that ranked 13 items did so, orally, by ranking items in subsets of 4 at at time (lambda one design).

Each set of items was read and the respondent was asked to choose one. Then, the remaining items were read and the respondent was asked to choose one. In this way, items in each subset were ordered in terms of preference and then the 13 subsets were combined to obtain a single rank order for each woman.

How to Do It

To create a BIB design, you must first decide what subset size (k) would be appropriate for your study. For similarity data, subsets of size three (triads) are appropriate. For ranking tasks, subset sizes of three or larger can be used. For orally administered ranking tasks, subset sizes should be limited to three or four.

Next, you must choose a BIB design. You must make sure that a "solution" exists for the number of items and the set size that you want. If you have 14 items and you want to collect triad similarity data, you must either drop or add one item, since there are no BIB triad designs for 14 items. With 13 items a lambda-one design with 26 triads can be created and with 15 items a lambda-one design with 35 triads can be created. Any of these designs are considerably shorter than the complete design. With many domains, the addition or deletion of an item poses no problem. Sometimes, however, a domain can consist of a fixed number of items, for example, in studying the social network of a group there may be a fixed number of people. In such a case, dummy items can be added; items that should clearly be at the bottom or at the top of any ranking. In a study of peer evaluations of clinical competency among 24 medical residents, Weller and Doughty (1985) added a name "Superdoc" to complete a design with 25 items ($k = 5$, $n = 25$, $b = 30$, $\lambda = 1$).

Since solutions do not exist for all values of n, λ , and k, Table 8.3 indicates many of the solutions for 30 or fewer items (Burton and Nerlove, 1976; Guilliksen and Tucker, 1961; Hall, 1967). Note that if a lambda-one design exists, a lambda-two, lambda-three design, and so on can be created by doubling or tripling the design and adding it to the original design. If a lambda-two design exists it can be doubled, creating a lambda-four design. Thus we have listed only the simpler (lambda-one, lambda-two) designs in Table 8.3. Although solutions exist in many sources, for example, combinatorics texts, we have reprinted some of the actual designs in Appendices C through I. Remember that a lambda-one design can be expanded into a lambda-two or higher design by randomizing your item numbers and then repeating the design.

If the design you desire has not been appended, you must generate the sets of items. Information to generate many of the triad solutions can be found in Burton and Nerlove (1976). For example, to generate a solution for 13 items where each pair appears only once (lambda-one), Burton and Nerlove give a solution from Cochran and Cox. Beginning with the base set 1, 4, 5, sets are generated by adding one to each number: 1, 4, 5; 2, 5, 6; 3, 6, 7; . . . 13, 3, 4. Note that since there are no numbers larger than 13, numbers begin again at 1 after 13. The second half of the design is generated in "cycle two" with the base set 1, 6, 8 adding 1 to each until the set 13, 5, 7 is reached. This completes the design with 26 sets of size three. To use the design, *randomize the order and position of items* (see chapter 5 on Triads).

The next step is to check your design. Make an N by N table. Using only the lower left or the upper right half of the table, put a mark in each cell, for every pair that occurs. If the first set is 1, 4, 5, the pairs 1, 4; 1, 5; and 4, 5 have occurred and should be marked with a one in the corresponding cells of the table. If you listed all the sets necessary and correctly for a lambda-one design, then each pair should appear once. In a lambda-two design, each pair should appear twice. Although with few items this does not seem necessary, it is highly recommended.

Interview data are collected by asking the informant either (1) to pick the most different item from each set of three (similarity data), or (2) to rank order the items in each subset. The triad similarity interview is straightforward whether done in a written or oral format. If the ranking interview is conducted orally, ranking is accomplished, for example, by reading all three items in a set and asking the informant to pick the one that they "like the most" or the one that is "the most X." Then the two remaining items in the set are reread and the question is asked again.

Tabulation

BIB triad similarity data are handled in the same way as complete triads (see Chapter 5 on Triads). Rank order data are tabulated by summing the ranks assigned to each item (see Chapter 7 on Rank Order Methods). The degree of inconsistency in a respondent's answers can be calculated from BIB rank order data collection tasks. Inconsistent or intransitive answers occur when someone says "A is more than B, B is more than C, and C is more than A." In fact, there are significance tests to test if a given respondent is answering significantly different from random (Guilliksen and Tucker, 1961; Weller, 1984b).

Strengths and Weaknesses

BIB designs can shorten and simplify a data collection task, allowing for the collection of data, orally or in written format, on larger numbers of items. Less information is collected per subject (as the number of paired comparisons decrease): (1) so that more subjects may be needed to get a stable estimate across subjects and (2) there is not enough data (especially, $\lambda = 1$) to perform a comparative analysis on individuals. In addition, lambda-one designs may be "unstable." Burton and Nerlove (1976) showed that lambda-one designs can produce artifactual results, if you happened to get an unusual randomization. However, Romney and Magaña (1977) showed two different randomizations, that is, two different (lambda-one) designs gave concordant results. The problem identified by Burton and Nerlove can be minimized by rerandomizing items between informants or between subsets of informants.

9. SENTENCE FRAME FORMATS

Sentence-frame substitutions facilitate the collection of data on related sets of items. Data collection with sentence frames begins by collecting lists of two related items. Typically, one list consists of a set of items and the second is a set of statements relevant to those items. Then, items are systematically paired with each statement. This is accomplished by creating "sentence frames" from the descriptive statements and substituting each item into each frame. Informant responses are usually represented in a table of items by characteristics. The interview tends to be quite lengthy, because two sets of items are compared. Nevertheless, sentence frame substitutions provide a unique data collection device that is flexible enough to be administered orally in remote and exotic settings or to be administered as a questionnaire to U.S. high school students or college undergraduates.

Examples

Although the use of sentence frames developed from methods in linguistics, they have been used most widely by anthropologists. Stefflre (1972) collected data regarding the beliefs about when to take medicines. Typical over-the-counter medicines and their possible uses were elicited in structured interviews. Fifty medicines and fifty uses were selected for further study. Descriptive sentence frames were created for each potential use and data were collected by systematically substituting each of the fifty medicines into each of the fifty sentence frames ($50 \times 50 =$ 2,500 questions). Informants were asked to judge the acceptability of each newly formed statement: "You take (*kind of medicine*) when you (*condition of use*)." The responses of a single informant appear in Table 9.1 (modified and adapted from Stefflre, 1972: 215). Positive responses were coded with ones and negative responses are blank. The informant judged the statement "You take *Contac* when *you have a runny nose*" to be acceptable, so the position in row one, last column, contains a one.

TABLE 9.1

	Hangover	*Earache*	*Hot and cold flashes*	*The children are sick*	*Fever*	*Wet and tired*	*The children have a fever*	*Taken a chill*	*After you've been ill*	*Going to be ill*	*Post-nasal drip*	*You have a cold*	*In the winter*	*The children have a cold*	*Laryngitis*	*Swollen glands*	*Tonsils are inflamed*	*Sore throat*	*During the flu season*	*The children are cranky*	*Asthma*	*Cough*	*Sore mouth*	*Bad taste in your mouth*	*Tightness in your chest*	*Sinus trouble*	*Stuffy head*	*Can't breathe*	*Stuffy nose*	*Can't breathe*	*Runny nose*
Contac												1	1	1	1				1							1	1	1	1	1	1
Vicks Sinex nasal spray												1	1													1	1	1	1	1	1
Privine nose drops												1	1													1	1	1	1	1	1
Neosynephrine nasal spray												1	1													1	1	1	1	1	1
Neosynephrine nose drops												1	1													1	1	1	1	1	1
Contac nasal mist												1	1													1	1	1	1	1	1
Privine nasal spray												1	1													1	1	1	1	1	1
Naso-dex												1	1	1												1	1	1	1	1	1
Dristan nasal decongestant capsules												1	1	1												1	1	1	1	1	1
Vicks inhaler											1	1	1	1					1							1	1	1	1	1	1
Dristan medicated room vaporizer						1					1	1	1	1							1	1			1	1	1	1	1	1	1
Metholatum												1	1	1							1	1			1	1	1	1	1	1	1
Vicks vapo-rub							1				1	1	1	1						1	1	1			1						
Adulton cough syrup											1	1	1								1	1			1						
Cough syrup											1	1	1	1	1					1	1	1			1						

Vicks formula 44 cough discs											1	1	1	1	1					1	1	1	1		1						
Romilar cough lozenges											1	1	1	1	1	1	1			1	1	1	1		1						
Vicks throat lozenges											1	1	1	1	1	1	1	1	1	1	1	1		1							
Spectrocin-T-troches											1	1	1	1	1	1	1	1	1	1	1	1	1	1							
Smith Brothers cough drops											1	1	1	1	1	1	1	1	1	1	1	1	1	1							
Vicks cough drops											1	1	1	1	1	1	1	1	1	1	1	1	1	1	1						
F & F cough drops											1	1	1	1	1	1	1	1	1	1	1	1	1	1	1						
Listerine throat lozenges											1	1	1	1	1	1	1	1	1	1	1	1	1	1							
Chloraseptic lozenges											1	1	1	1	1	1	1	1	1	1	1	1	1								
Cepacol throat lozenges											1	1	1	1	1	1	1	1	1	1	1	1		1							
F & F lozenges											1	1	1	1	1	1	1	1	1	1	1	1		1							
Sucrets												1	1	1	1	1	1	1		1		1		1							
Salt water gargle	1										1	1	1		1	1	1	1				1									
Seeing the doctor		1	1	1	1			1	1	1		1		1	1	1	1	1	1		1										
Calling the doctor		1	1	1	1		1	1		1		1	1	1	1	1	1	1	1	1	1	1									
Bufferin	1	1	1	1	1	1	1	1	1	1		1	1	1	1	1	1	1	1	1	1										
Anacin	1	1	1	1	1	1	1	1	1	1	1	1	1	1	1	1	1	1	1	1	1										
Aspirin	1	1	1	1	1	1	1	1	1	1	1	1	1	1	1	1	1	1	1	1	1										
Empirin compound	1	1	1	1	1	1	1	1	1	1	1	1	1	1	1	1	1	1	1	1	1										
Excedrin	1	1	1	1	1	1	1	1	1	1	1	1	1	1	1	1	1	1	1	1	1										
A.P.C. tablets		1		1	1	1	1	1	1	1	1	1	1	1	1	1	1	1	1	1	1										
Hot lemonade			1	1	1	1	1	1	1	1	1	1	1	1	1	1	1	1	1	1	1	1		1	1	1	1	1	1	1	1
Hot tea		1	1	1	1	1	1	1	1	1	1	1	1	1	1	1	1	1	1	1	1	1	1	1	1	1	1	1	1	1	1
A hot toddy	1	1	1		1	1		1	1		1	1	1		1	1	1	1	1		1	1	1		1	1	1		1	1	
Coricidin cold tablets			1			1	1	1	1	1	1	1	1	1	1		1	1	1	1					1						1
Vitamins	1			1		1	1	1	1	1		1	1	1	1	1	1		1	1											

SOURCE: Stefflre (1972: 222-223). Reprinted by permission.

Since both the medicines and their uses focus primarily on cold and flu remedies we can see this subject's beliefs about how to treat a cold. For example, in the upper right hand corner there is a cluster of related symptoms and medicines: The informant reported that nose drops, sprays, mists, and inhalers are appropriate for sinus trouble, a stuffy head, or a stuffy nose. Syrups, lozenges, and cough drops are judged to be appropriate for inflamed throat and glands.

Fabrega (1970) used sentence frame substitutions as an exploratory device to discover the cultural meaning of illness terms. In the Mayan Indian community of Zinacantan, Chiapas, Mexico, he compared the illness beliefs of 30 curers and 30 noncurers. Each person was asked a series of questions in the Tzotzil dialect, comparing 18 illness terms with 24 potential body disturbances (symptoms). Illness terms were chosen to represent a cross section of Zinacantan folk illnesses, referring to "different body abnormalities," "morality," and "social processes." The signs and symptoms referred to behavioral events and disturbances in bodily processes that represented "meaningful units of Zinacantan discourse regarding behavior and bodily concerns" (p. 307). Each person was asked whether "each of the 24 potential illness manifestations constituted an element of each of the various illness terms" (p. 307). Using the distribution of affirmative responses across concepts, Fabrega identified concepts that characterized Zinacantan concepts of illness.

D'Andrade et al. (1972) also used sentence substitutions to study concepts of disease. In a cross-cultural study, they examined English-speaking American and Spanish-speaking Mexican categorization of diseases. American-English disease terms were selected by composing lists of common diseases and asking informants to select the most common and least ambiguous terms. Using both the investigators' and the informants' folk knowledge about illness, lists of "properties" relevant to illness, that is, statements about illness, were generated. Sentence frames were created from the list of properties in a form "approximating ordinary usage," for example, contagion was expressed as "You can catch ______ from other people" (p. 13).

Since many of the statements appeared to be rephrasings of the same or similar propositions, the list of statements was shortened, including statements that were relatively independent and not too specific. Since there are no clear-cut rules about inclusion and exclusion of sentence frames, D'Andrade et al. noted that

> reliance must be placed on informants' judgments and on the . . . analysis . . . [Bad items can be] identified as poor choices in the course of the analysis itself and then removed. In general, poor items show wide varia-

> tion in response from individual to individual, little variation across items, and tend to be used differently by the same individual at different times [p. 13].

After assembling lists of diseases and properties, D'Andrade et al. then conducted a pretest in English. In the final study, 38 disease terms were compared with 38 sentence frames (38 × 38 = 1,444 questions); and 56 disease terms were compared with 56 disease properties (3,136 questions) for the Mexican sample. Each disease was substituted into every sentence frame and informants were asked whether or not the newly formed sentence was true or false. Questions were administered orally to the Mexicans, requesting yes/no responses. Because of the length of the interview, Mexican interviews were conducted in more than one session and informants were paid according to local rates. The American sample filled out a written form, rating each statement on a 5-point scale from "definitely" to "definitely not." Responses greater than 3.5 were recoded as yes's as those below 3.5 as no's. Responses of informants in each group were summed into a single table, and recoded into yes's (ones) if the value was greater than the mean and to no's (blanks) if it was less than the mean. The disease properties appear in Table 9.2. The responses of 10 English-speaking undergraduates from Stanford University appear in Table 9.3. The table has been rearranged with the aid of hierarchical clustering and subgroupings or clusters of diseases and properties are superimposed on the table. Clusters of diseases are positioned with horizontal lines and property clusters are partitioned with vertical lines. For the American sample, there are two major categories of disease each with three subcategories. The first major category includes the diseases from "tonsillitis" down to "typhoid fever" (diseases that are contagious and tend to affect children; acute conditions). For example, the majority of informants believed that "Most people catch tonsillitis in bad weather," that a "Sore throat comes with tonsillitis," and so on. The second category includes "gonnorhea" down to "rheumatism" (diseases that tend to be more severe, affecting adults; chronic conditions).

How to Do It

Sentence frame substitution interviews or questionnaires are prepared by first eliciting domain items and their attributes, features, causes, or uses. For oral presentations, a table of items by attribute frames can be created with items being represented as rows and attributes as columns (or vice versa). Then, each item is paired with each attribute in a grammatically correct statement and each informant is asked if that

TABLE 9.2
American-English Belief Frames

(1) You can catch __________ from other people.
(2) __________ is caused by germs.
(3) Most people catch __________ in bad weather.
(4) __________ comes from being emotionally upset.
(5) __________ runs in the family.
(6) When you are overtired, your resistance to __________ is lowered.
(7) __________ can't be cured.
(8) __________ has to run its course.
(9) __________ should be treated with miracle drugs.
(10) __________ gets better by itself.
(11) __________ is serious.
(12) __________ is a fatal disease.
(13) You never really get over __________.
(14) __________ is a crippling disease.
(15) You can have __________ and not know it.
(16) __________ spreads through your whole system.
(17) __________ is contagious.
(18) If a woman comes down with __________ during her pregnancy, it harms her child.
(19) Feeling generally run-down is a sign of __________.
(20) __________ affects the heart.
(21) Your skin breaks out with __________.
(22) Runny nose is a sign of __________.
(23) Sore throat comes with __________.
(24) __________ brings on fever.
(25) Once you've had __________, you can't get it again.
(26) __________ is a children's disease.
(27) Most people get __________ at one time or other.
(28) Some people have a tendency to get __________.
(29) It's safer to have __________ as a child and get it over with.
(30) __________ is a sign of old age.

SOURCE: D'Andrade et al. (1972: 12). Reprinted by permission.

statement makes sense or is true. Answers are recorded as 0 for no or false and 1 for positive responses. For questionnaires or written presentations each statement should be written out in full with yes/no or true/false choices. The responses of each individual are tabulated into a table and, typically, the responses of all subjects are added together into one table (Fabrega, 1970; Stefflre, 1972; D'Andrade et al., 1972; Young, 1978).

Variations

Sentence frames may be collected orally or in a written format. Responses are usually coded dichotomously, although D'Andrade et al. used a rating scale and later recoded the responses into dichotomous categories. Most variations, however, occur in the analysis. Fabrega (1970) tallied responses and interpreted responses with greater than 80% agreement. D'Andrade et al. (1972), Stefflre (1972), Young (1978), and Weller et al. (1987) rearranged the order of the rows and columns with hierarchical clustering to aid in identifying clusters of items and their attributes. Weller et al. (1987) and Garro (1986) examined variability among individuals' response tables. In studies that used hierarchical clustering to reorder rows and columns, similarity was first derived between all pairs of diseases (rows) based on the degree to which they shared common attributes (columns) and between all pairs of attributes (columns) based on the degree to which they co-occur in the same diseases (rows). Sentence substitution data may also be examined in detail to discover which attributes are essential in defining an item. Bruner et al. (1965: 30-40) refer to attributes with a strong relation to an item "criterial attributes." D'Andrade (1976) and Young (1978) examined the criteriality of properties of disease (the sentence frames) to describe cause-and-effect beliefs regarding diseases.

Strengths and Weaknesses

Sentence frame substitutions facilitate the collection of systematic data linking two related domains. Similarity data among items can be derived from the pattern of shared attributes. Sentence frame data also lends itself to a propositional analysis (cause-and-effect beliefs). The main disadvantage is that it can be a long and boring task, taking multiple sessions to complete one interview.

Although the interview may be extremely long (Stefflre et al. [1971] used approximately 2,500 questions per informant), the data appear to be reliable. If such a long interview elicited "random" or meaningless responses (as suggested by Foster, 1979), then responses of pairs of informants would be unrelated or uncorrelated. However, Weller et al. (1987), with 135 questions, found responses to be quite reliable with interinformant correlations to be about .45. Stefflre et al. compared the

TABLE 9.3

Distributional Patterning Based on Hierarchical Clustering for American Sample

		WEATHR 3	THROAT 23	FEVER 24	ITSELF 10	NOSE 22	RESIST 6	CATCH 1	CONTAG 17	GERMS 2	DRUGS 9	ONCR 25	SAFECH 29	CHILDR 26	MOST 27	SPREAD 16	RUNDOW 19	PREGNA 18	COURSE 8	SERIOU 11	FATAL 12	HEART 20	SKIN 21	INHERI 5	NEVER 13	NOCURE 7	CRIPPL 14	TENDEN 28	OLDAGE 30	ENOTNL 4	NOTKNO 15
tonsillitis	26	x	x	x			x			x		x	x	x	x																x
appendicitis	1			x								x	x		x					x	x										x
poison ivy	18				x			x	x						x				x				x					x			
strep throat	23	x	x	x	x		x	x	x	x	x			x	x				x												
laryngitis	11	x	x	x	x		x	x	x	x	x			x	x				x									x			
whooping cough	30	x	x	x	x	x	x	x	x	x	x	x	x	x				x			x										
influenza	10	x	x	x	x	x	x	x	x	x	x				x	x	x	x	x												
pneumonia	17	x	x	x	x	x	x	x	x	x	x					x	x	x	x	x	x										
mononucleosis	15	x		x	x	x	x	x	x	x	x					x	x	x	x			x									x
a cold	5	x	x	x	x	x	x	x	x	x					x	x	x		x							x		x			x
bronchitis	2	x	x	x	x	x	x		x	x	x									x								x	x		x

chicken pox	4			x	x		x	x	x	x	x	x	x	x	x	x		x	x				x								
measles	14			x	x	x	x	x	x	x		x	x	x	x	x		x	x												
mumps	16		x	x	x		x	x	x	x		x	x	x	x	x	x	x	x												
smallpox	22			x				x	x	x	x	x	x	x		x		x	x	x	x		x								
typhoid fever	28	x		x			x	x	x	x	x	x	x	x		x		x	x	x	x										
gonorrhea	8							x	x	x	x							x		x	x		x				x				x
syphilis	25							x	x	x	x					x		x		x	x	x	x				x				x
polio	19							x	x	x	x	x		x		x	x	x	x	x	x	x			x	x	x				
leukemia	12										x	x		x		x	x	x	x	x	x	x		x	x	x	x				x
tuberculosis	27						x	x	x	x	x	x				x	x	x	x	x	x				x	x					x
malaria	13			x						x	x					x	x	x		x	x	x			x						
stroke	24						x									x		x	x	x	x	x		x	x	x	x	x	x	x	
heart attack	9						x											x	x	x	x	x		x	x	x	x	x	x	x	x
cancer	3															x	x	x		x	x	x	x	x	x	x	x	x	x		x
psychosis	20						x													x				x	x	x	x	x	x	x	x
ulcers	29																							x	x			x	x	x	x
epilepsy	7													x						x				x	x	x	x			x	x
dental cavities	6														x									x	x	x		x			x
rheumatism	21	x									x					x	x		x					x	x	x	x	x	x		x

SOURCE: D'Andrade et al. (1972: 30). Reprinted by permission.

responses of pairs of informants and found the similarity between items to be quite high across informants (correlations ranged between .77 and .89).

10. OTHER COMMON STRUCTURED FORMATS: DICHOTOMOUS, MULTIPLE CHOICE, FILL-IN-THE-BLANK, MATCHING, DIRECT ESTIMATION, AND PICK N

There are a number of common formats that have not yet been discussed in detail. For a variety of reasons we have chosen not to devote a complete chapter on each. Some of the formats, *dichotomous,* for example, are basically so simple and familiar that they do not really need extended treatment. Others, such as matching, are not used very frequently and examples of their use in the literature are seldom found. The various formats are discussed in turn and the fact that they are all covered in a single chapter should not be interpreted as meaning that there is some conceptual coherence among the formats. They are grouped here solely as a matter of convenience.

The Dichotomous Format

The dichotomous format is actually any question that can be answered with a dichotomous response: true/false, yes/no, agree/disagree, hot/cold, and so on. It is also a special case of a rating scale, for example, a "two-point" rating scale and a special case of a multiple-choice format. The dichotomous format is widely used in social science questionnaires. The format is very flexible and can be used in a great many different ways. It is frequently used in classrooms as a device to find out how much of the material presented has been learned by the students. Personality inventories typically request dichotomous responses, usually in a checklist form (where checks indicate "true" and blanks indicate "false"). For example, the Minnesota Multiphasic Personality Inventory (Dahlstrom et al., 1975) uses 550 true-false questions about beliefs and attitudes of the respondent. Both of these uses are designed to assess some aspect of the respondents, whether the purpose is classroom knowledge or a "psychological profile." Answers to these types of tests typically are coded by the researcher as "correct-incorrect" or "appropriate-inappropriate," since the "correct" answers are known when the questions are asked.

Another context in which dichotomous questions are useful is in situations where the answers are not known ahead of time. The answers to the questions may in fact be the major interest of the researcher. In one such study, Garro (1987) was interested in characterizing a "prototypic" set of beliefs that an Athabascan Indian group held concerning "hypertension." She collected a number of possible beliefs from free interviewing and then presented them to a sample of Indians in true-false format. She coded the answers in terms of "response" data, that is, how they were actually answered by the informants. She then analyzed them in terms of consensus analysis (see Chapter 11 for details) to estimate the culturally correct answer to each question.

Another study in which the true-false format was used to investigate the existence of a culturally defined set of beliefs about the use of hot or cold medicines in the treatment of disease may be found in Weller's (1983) work on the hot-cold concept of illness in Guatemala. In the collection of one set of data

> 16 women were asked to classify each of the disease terms as needing either hot or cold remedies or medicines. The list of disease terms was read, and for each term the informant was asked, "Does ______ need hot remedies or medicines?" When the list was completed, the list was reread, and the informant was asked for each term, "Does ______ need cold remedies or medicines?" This was done to identify informants who were not giving consistent or meaningful answers, for example, those who gave all "yes" or "no" responses [Weller, 1983: 252].

There are two items of special note on this example. One is the repeat of the question in both the "hot" direction and the "cold" direction as a kind of check on severe response bias. In field studies where communication difficulties are possible it is probably a very good idea to use all the checks that one can design into the interview.

The second and more general characteristic of the hot-cold example has to do with asking the same true-false question about each of several items in a domain, in this case the list of illnesses. By using the same format on another concept, namely, contagion, Weller (1983) was able to show that the structure of responses for hot-cold were very different than the structure of responses for contagion.

It should be noted that the use of sentence frames as described in the previous chapter are a variant of the dichotomous format. A sentence frame interview format can be considered as simply one very long true-false instrument. Sentence frames, however, allow the analysis of the characteristics of both the beliefs (e.g., symptoms) and the items (e.g., illnesses).

Multiple-Choice Format

The primary use of multiple-choice formats in social science is probably in the construction of tests of ability and aptitude. Such well-known tests as the GRE (Graduate Record Examination) and SAT (Scholastic Aptitude Test) are two examples of a large number of such tests. Aptitude test answers are always known ahead of time and thus responses are coded as correct-incorrect.

Multiple-choice questions contain more "information" than do dichotomous questions. This is true because of "guessing." In a true-false question one can get the correct answer half of the time by guessing. In a multiple-choice question with four possible answers one can get the correct answer only a quarter of the time by guessing.

Since each multiple-choice question contains more information about how much ability a subject has than does a true-false question the test instrument can be shorter. Thus the wide use of multiple-choice tests for ability and aptitude testing. One difficulty with multiple-choice items is the creation of "filler" alternatives that are equally attractive. The writing and testing of such alternatives is both difficult and expensive and involves a great deal of research. This is why they are generally prepared by large organizations that specialize in the preparation of such tests.

In some cases there may be a small number of known alternatives to a set of systematic questions in which case the multiple-choice format is appropriate. One example of such a situation is in a study by Sankoff (1971). In this study, Sankoff was studying the ownership of land. Each plot of land in the society she was studying was in the hands of one or the other of six clans. For each plot of land she asked the question that could be phrased as, "Which of the six clans does this plot belong to?"

Fill-in-the-Blank Type Formats

The fill-in-the-blank format is closely related to the above two types of formats, and in some ways is a natural extension. Suppose, for example, we ask a question such as, "Who was president of the United States when the Interstate Freeway system was initiated?" The format is a fill-in-the-blank type although it resembles the multiple choice in that if one knew the names of presidents of this century the task is to choose among them. In the Sankoff example discussed above we classified the question about clans as a multiple-choice question since we were willing to assume that every informant knew the names of all six clans and was simply choosing among them. Of course if the number of alternatives becomes large then we think of the question as a fill-in-the-blank type format.

The amount of information collected per question is a function of the number of possible responses. Thus the amount of information in a fill-in-the-blank question is greater than a multiple-choice question and a multiple-choice question requests "more" information than a dichotomous question. This is true because guessing an answer becomes less likely as the number of possibilities increases. In some preliminary studies we carried out it was found that one fill-in-the-blank question had as much "information" as five dichotomous questions. This means that fewer fill-in-the-blank questions are needed to reach the same degree of reliability.

Teachers use fill-in-the-blank questions on tests. The format is also a natural one for eliciting information from informants where the aim is to find out new information. In searching the literature for examples of where the method has been used to elicit information we get the impression that the method is very widespread for informal use. For example, ethnographers would use it almost without thinking to ask questions such as, "What is that?" pointing to a strange flower or food or whatever. What is lacking in most cases is the systematic application of the technique so that a sample of informants is presented with the same set of questions.

A particularly apt use of the format, that deserves wide adaptation, comes from some ethnographic data collected by Boster (1985) on Aguaruna manioc classification. He collected several dozen varieties of manioc and planted them in a garden. When the plants matured he asked informants to identify the growing manioc plants in the garden. "Data were collected by guiding informants through the gardens, stopping at each plant and asking, 'What kind of manioc is this?' " (Boster, 1985: 180). This provided Boster (1985, 1986b) with a powerful set of data that yielded some very interesting results and generalizations. The highlights of his analysis include the following findings: The data revealed that the more subjects agreed with each other the more knowledge they had about manioc. He was able to establish both the "culturally" defined correct name of each plant and the cultural knowledge of each informant. This allowed him to demonstrate that women knew more than men about manioc culture. He also showed that women in the same kin and residential groups were more similar to each other in cultural knowledge than nonrelated women.

Boster also asked the same questions of the same informants on two separate occasions and found that the informants who were most consistent were the same informants who had the highest cultural knowledge overall. This use of the fill-in-the-blank format illustrates an optimal use of a structured interview design. The arrangement of the interviewing situation was natural to the subjects, the task has high face validity and the format lends itself to both simple and sophisticated analyses.

Matching Formats

In presenting a matching task format, informants are normally presented with two lists that are linked in some way but are scrambled in presentation. The task is to match items from one list with items on another list. For example, historic figures might be matched to their birth dates. This format is frequently use in classroom test situations since it is easy to make up questions in a short time. It is not frequently used in formal research situations. There are probably some situations in which it would be very useful.

Estimation Formats

The use of estimation procedures is frequently overlooked partly because in the cases where they might be used one could measure the variable under consideration directly and not elicit the information from informants. For example, if one were interested in how tall people are, the natural thing would be actually to measure their height. However, estimates of height or distance are of value precisely because they can be validated and informant accuracy can be assessed. Thus estimates can serve as benchmarks to compare different data collection techniques.

These ideas have been used in the analysis of environmental cognition data. Magana et al. (1981) studied judgments of distances among buildings on a university campus. In their study, the basic purpose was to compare the accuracy of several different cognitive mapping methodologies. They used four data collection methods: (1) an unconstrained cognitive mapping task that consisted of asking subjects to draw a map of the campus; (2) a constrained mapping task in which subjects were asked to draw a map of the campus but were told which elements to include; (3) estimations of distances between specified buildings; (4) a triads task using combinations of building in the task and asking which was furthest from the other two. The researchers also measured the actual distances among buildings. For the estimation task, undergraduate students who had been enrolled for a minimum of two years were asked to estimate the distance between all possible pairs of buildings. The students were told that they could use whatever system of units was easiest (feet, meters, yards). The estimates from all four tasks were highly correlated with the actual distances.

In a series of informal classroom experiments with variables that could be validated, for example, height, we have found that people are very good at estimation tasks. We feel that they could be used in a wider variety of situations than has been true in the past.

The Pick N Format

In various guises this format has already been covered. For example, the triad task of picking "the item most different from the other two" is a pick one of three type format. Multiple-choice questions are a pick one of n (usually four) type. In early sociometric studies it was typical to ask subjects to pick their three best friends from a class list. Nowadays in sociometric studies we strongly recommend the use of complete rank ordering of preferences if at all possible. In cases where this is not possible, it is probably best to pick about half the stimuli, instead of choosing three. More information is contained in such a split than in the case where one picks only a few items.

Krackhardt and Kilduff (1987) used a pick n format for collecting sociometric data. Krackhardt and Kilduff were interested not only in each person's "friends" but also in their perception of the friends of others, so each informant identified their friends on a list of 48 and then identified who they thought the friends of each of those 48 people were. Because of the length of the questionnaire a ranking task was not feasible. Instead, they choose a checklist format in which each informant "picked" individuals by putting a mark by their name in the list.

11. RELIABILITY, CONSENSUS, AND SAMPLE SIZE

In the previous chapters we have reviewed a number of possible formats for the collection of data in structured interviews. In the final two chapters we turn to questions related to reliability and validity. A potential user of the methods will want to know how reliable the results are likely to be in terms of consistency. One would also want to know whether measures derived from the use of these formats had validity in the sense that they measured what one thought one was measuring.

In this chapter we summarize what is known about measuring the reliability and the stability of results of a single sample of structured interviews. This includes what is usually covered in discussions of sample size and reliability. We add to this recent findings about consensus among subjects that provide new tools for the analysis of how much confidence to place in the results of structured interviewing techniques. In the next chapter we turn to the question of validity and how to increase our confidence in the overall results of research by replication and related techniques.

In the simplest terms, reliability is synonymous with consistency. It is the degree to which an instrument, a test, a questionnaire, or an interview can retrieve the same answers when applied under similar conditions. A common index of reliability is a test-retest reliability. Can a test retrieve similar scores when given to the same individuals on two different occasions? Unfortunately, with interviews or tests given to human beings, there can be learning effects and memory biases that influence their performance from one time to another. Thus reliability measured on a test-retest basis can be distorted. A conceptually related measure, which is not sensitive to learning effects because it is obtained from a single sample, is split-half reliability. If we sampled questions at random from one domain, they would be representative of all possible questions from that domain. If the sample of questions were randomly divided into two subsamples, each would be representative of the larger population and hence the answers or "scores" from each subsample would be similar if the "test" were reliable.

A more powerful and therefore preferable measure is the reliability coefficient, sometimes called Chronbach's alpha. The reliability coefficient is relatively simple to compute and is equivalent to calculating all possible split-half reliabilities without actually having to do so. When conducting an analysis of *item* reliability, the square root of the reliability coefficient estimates the correlation of empirically obtained scores with the true unobservable scores. When analyzing the reliability of *informants*, the square root of the reliability coefficient provides an estimate of the correlation of the actual responses with the true answers, for example, it provides an estimate of the validity of informants' responses. The reliability coefficient is "so pregnant with meaning that it should be routinely applied to all new tests" (Nunnally, 1978: 214).

We would like to stress here, however, the difference between the traditional psychological approach in testing theory and the approach of the ethnographer. In test theory, it is assumed that the answers to questions are known beforehand. Thus informants' responses can be coded as "correct" or "incorrect." Item analysis or an analysis of item reliability presupposes that responses have been coded as correct and incorrect. In contrast, the ethnographer does not know what the answers are or what they should be and, instead, is trying to discover the "culturally correct" responses. An analysis of "informant reliability" provides optimal estimates of the culturally correct answers. It is like an item analysis except that the raw, uncoded responses are used and the analysis focuses on people rather than items. It is this latter type of "reliability" analysis (How do I know when I have the "right" answers?) that is related to test theory but comes from the consensus model, with which the ethnographer is concerned. Thus the two approaches are appropriate under different circumstances and provide different information.

In this chapter, we describe both item reliability and the consensus model. Because the study of consensus is new and is related to reliability theory in general, we begin by describing item reliability. A major aim of the chapter is to introduce the Spearman-Brown Prophesy Formula and to show how it applies to both items and informants. It is from the Spearman-Brown Prophesy Formula that one can calculate: (1) the optimal number of test questions to create a reliable test, or (2) the necessary number of informants to obtain reliable answers in an interview.

Item Reliability

In the broadest sense, we use structured interviewing techniques in order to measure something of interest about either the people being interviewed or about the items of information contained in the questions. Traditional reliability measures were developed to measure the ability of items to distinguish among individuals. For example, intelligence tests are made up of a large set of items, each one of which is an indicator of intelligence. The test is designed to distinguish individuals in terms of how intelligent they are as measured by the test. In this section we will present the current model of reliability as developed by test theory researchers over the last century. In the next section we will show how the results can be applied to measuring the reliability of the information content of the interview, that is, how well the informants can distinguish among items of information.

The model of item reliability that we present here is called the domain-sampling model. (A technical discussion can be found in Nunnally, 1978). The model assumes that each response is coded as correct or incorrect. Items or questions are selected from the universe of test questions that form a single coherent domain, for example, questions that measure some ability such as spelling. Each question (in this case, a word to be spelled) is seen as being a sample indicator of an underlying ability to spell. A specific test of an ability is viewed as containing a random sample of items from the universe of all relevant questions. One could construct any number of tests of spelling by drawing different random samples of items (words) to include in the various tests. The reliability of any of the tests constructed in this way is defined as the expected correlation of scores on a specific test with scores on another test of the same length constructed in the same way. In other words, it is the correlation between any two tests constructed by random selection of equal number of items from the universe of all possible items.

The domain-sampling model of reliability is based on a number of assumptions. The first assumption is that each item or question is a positive, although imperfect, indicator of the ability under consideration. That is, if we are measuring spelling ability we assume that each possible word in the universe is an indicator of spelling ability. An implication of this is that if we actually knew the true ability of the informants, each item would have a positive correlation with the true ability of the informants. That is, a higher proportion of high-ability subjects than low-ability subjects would get each item correct.

A second assumption is that each item is "locally independent" of every other item. Independence among items implies that each item contributes separate information about ability. Thus the more items there are in a test, the greater the reliability of the test, as additional items add more information. Another implication is that the correlation among items is brought about solely as the result of each item's correlation with the true scores. Items that are highly correlated with the underlying trait or ability will be highly correlated with each other. In fact, the correlation between two items *i* and *j* (r_{ij}) is the product of the correlation between each item and the underlying trait or ability: $r_{ij} = r_{it}r_{jt}$. It should make sense that items in a test of ability should correlate with each other since otherwise the items could not possibly be measuring the same thing.

The Spearman-Brown Prophesy Formula (Nunnally, 1978: 211) summarizes the above discussion. The reliability (r_{kk}) of a test is a function of the number of items (k) and the average intercorrelation among those items ($\bar{r}_{ij}$):

$$r_{kk} = \frac{k \cdot \bar{r}_{ij}}{1 + (k - 1)\bar{r}_{ij}}$$

The reliability coefficient, r_{kk} has a straightforward interpretation. It is the expected correlation between any two tests of equal length. Also, the square root of the reliability coefficient is an estimate of the correlation between the empirical test scores and the true scores. For example, a 30-item test with a .20 average correlation among items would have a reliability coefficient of .88. Thus the test would be expected to correlate about .88 with another test made up of a different random sample of 30 items from the same domain or universe of items and the scores obtained from this test would be expected to correlate .94 (the square root of .88) with the true scores. One can see that the formula allows one to aggregate the contributions of each item into a single prediction or "prophesy" of how the test correlates with the "true scores."

A fascinating feature of the Spearman-Brown formula is that it works regardless of the size of the "units" that are added. The average correlation among units, whether those units are items or tests, is all that needs to be known. The notion of adding units of different sizes can be illustrated by considering two equivalent tests of size 15 rather than a single test of 30 items as in the above example. A 15-item test with an average intercorrelation among items of .20 would have a reliability coefficient of .789. If we added together two tests or "units" of 15 items each with an average intercorrelation of .789 between them we would get a reliability coefficient of .88, the same as with a single test with 30 items.

These results depend, of course, upon the assumption that the items are all randomly drawn from a universe of items representing the same domain. The main way to test the reasonableness of this assumption is to determine whether the items are all positively correlated with each other. If they are not then one cannot expect that the model will give accurate results.

A reliability analysis usually includes the calculation of the reliability coefficient with the Spearman-Brown Formula. In addition, the reliability of each item can be estimated by correlating the responses from all informants for *a given item* with the summed responses for *all other items* ("item-total" correlation). In any serious research work one should always apply it to any new measure derived from test results coded correct or incorrect. Although a reliability analysis can be conducted by hand, statistical computing programs such as SPSSX (SPSS Inc.) contain procedures to analyze item reliability.

Consensus Theory

We turn now to the situation in which the answers to the questions are not known ahead of time. Therefore reliability theory as presented in the last section cannot be used since that theory as presented depends upon coding the questions as "correct" or "incorrect." Consensus theory allows us to measure the competence of each informant and to reconstruct the correct answers with about as much assurance as if we had the actual answers. The consensus model parallels the reasoning and formulas of reliability theory with two very important differences.

The first critical difference is that "response" data rather than "performance" data are used. This means that the data are coded as given by the respondent and are NOT recoded as "correct" or "incorrect" by the researcher. In the discussions to follow, it will be easiest to think of a true-false format although the theory will handle other formats as well, for example, multiple-choice, fill-in-the-blank, rank order, interval estimates, and matching formats. In a typical application for true-false data, if the informant answers "true" we would code the response "1" while if the informant answers "false" we would code the response "0." Note that this differs from "performance" data where the code "1" would indicate that the subject answered "correctly" (regardless of whether the response was "true" or "false") and the code "0" would indicate that the subject answered "incorrectly."

The second critical difference is that the role of the subjects and items are reversed. In reliability theory we think of a universe of items while in consensus theory we think of a universe of informants. Whereas in reliability theory we view the items as assessing the "competence" of the individual, for example, how smart or how good at spelling, in consensus theory we view the informants as providing information on a set of questions. In most of this book it has been assumed that we are interested in finding out what the informants know about some subject matter. We want to be able to estimate how much each informant knows and how to put the answers of the various informants together in order to arrive at some composite picture of what they know. Consensus theory provides a way of performing these tasks.

The technical details of consensus analysis can be found elsewhere (Batchelder and Romney, 1986; Romney, Weller, and Batchelder, 1986; Romney and Weller, 1984; Romney, Batchelder, and Weller, 1987; Weller, 1984b, 1987). Here we will present an informal intuitive description that will provide insight into how it works and what it does. The first assumption of consensus theory is that each informant has some knowledge of the subject matter contained in the structured interview. This exactly parallels the assumption in reliability theory that the item is an indicator of the ability under consideration. As in reliability theory, this assumption implies that if the answers to the questions were known, each informant's responses would have a positive correlation with the correct answers. Thus the central idea of consensus theory is the use of the pattern of agreement or consensus among informants to make inferences about their knowledge of the answers to the questions.

A central assumption of the consensus model is that the correspondence between any two informants is a function of the extent to which each has knowledge of the culturally correct answers. In the discussion of item reliability we noted that the correlation between two items is the product of their independent correlations with the true underlying trait or ability ($r_{ij} = r_{it}\ r_{jt}$). In consensus analysis the same assumption is applied to informants. Here, however, the formula expresses the central assumption that the correlation between two informants, *i* and *j*, is a function of the extent to which each is correlated with or has knowledge of the "truth," for example, the culturally correct answers.

Suppose, for example, that we have a set of interview questions concerning the game of tennis. If we interviewed tennis players and non-tennis players, we would expect that the tennis players would agree more among themselves as to the answers to the various questions than would the non-tennis players. Players that are knowledgeable about the game would answer more questions correctly, and therefore respond similarly, while players with little knowledge of the game would give answers that were different from each other as well as the better players. Thus we can figure out how much each person knows from the pattern of correlations among people.

Once we know how much each informant knows we can figure out the answers to the questions by weighting each informant's input and aggregating to estimate the most likely answer. Those who want to use the most exact methods should consult the sources cited above. Below we outline a very good method that is easily available and will serve for almost all purposes.

A consensus analysis is a kind of reliability analysis performed on people instead of items. Because of this, widely available statistical packages such as SPSS can be used for both reliability analysis on items and a consensus analysis on informants. In a reliability analysis, items are variables and informants are cases. Data are coded as PERFORMANCE data, that is, a 1 for "correct" and a 0 for "incorrect." In a consensus analysis, people and items are transposed: informants are variables and items are cases. The data must be coded as RESPONSE data, that is, a 1 if the informant said yes and a 0 if the informant said no. Consensus analysis can be performed on most structured interview data. Response data can be dichotomous (yes/no, hot/cold, and so on), ordered (rating scales, rank orders, even ranked pairs), or interval type data.

The Spearman-Brown Prophesy Formula and the reliability coefficient can be reinterpreted for informants (Weller, 1987). The reliability of informants can be calculated from the average intercorrelation *among respondents* ($\bar{r}_{ij}$) and the number *of respondents* (k). (Refer to the Spearman-Brown Prophesy Formula above.) Thus reliability of a set of responses is a function of the degree of agreement among respondents and the number of respondents. The square root of the reliability coefficient estimates the validity of the aggregated responses, that is, it is an estimate of the correlation between the "true" or culturally correct answers and the empirically obtained answers. When answers are a simple aggregate (unweighted average), the estimated validity (square root of the reliability coefficient) can be calculated from the agreement among respondents (average intercorrelation) and the number of respondents (see Table 11.1, adapted from Weller, 1987). For example, if you interviewed 17 informants and noted an average intercorrelation of .36 in their responses, and aggregation of those responses should correlate approximately .95 with the true answers.

In interviewing on the content of cultural patterns it is not unusual that the average correlation among subjects is .5 or higher since there is generally high agreement about what the answers are and each subject knows the majority of the answers. For this reason one does not usually need large samples to infer the answers.

The number of informants necessary to produce various levels of confidence (for dichotomous data) can also be calculated with the formal consensus model (Romney, Weller, and Batchelder, 1986). To do so, the average knowledge or competence of the informants (the "reliability" of each individual) is needed as well as the proportion of questions to be classified correctly, and the level of confidence that items have been correctly classified. Table 11.2 shows the number of informants needed for 95% and 99% confidence levels. It lists competence levels from .5 to .9 in steps of .1 along the columns. (Competency is equivalent to the square root of the average intercorrelation among informants.) The row headings are the lowest acceptable proportion of questions that will be decisively classified given various row and column choices. The numbers in the body of the table report the minimal number of informants needed to reach the levels specified.

For example, assume that you calculated the average competence among the informants and found it to be .6. If you wanted to classify at least 90% of questions correctly at the .95 level of confidence, reference to Table 11.2 shows the number 9. This means that with an average

TABLE 11.1
Agreement Among Individuals and Estimated Validity of Aggregating Their Responses for Different Sample Sizes

	Validity				
Agreement	.80	.85	.90	.95	.99
.16	10	14	22	49	257
.25	5	8	13	28	148
.36	3	5	8	17	87
.49	2	3	4	10	51

TABLE 11.2
Minimal Number of Informants Needed to Classify a Desired Proportion of Questions with a Specified Confidence Level for Different Levels of Cultural Competence

Proportion	*Average Level of Cultural Competence*				
of Questions	*.5*	*.6*	*.7*	*.8*	*.9*
.95 Confidence Level					
.80	9	7	4	4	4
.85	11	7	4	4	4
.90	13	9	6	4	4
.95	17	11	6	6	4
.99	29	19	10	8	4
.99 Confidence Level					
.80	15	10	5	4	4
.85	15	10	7	5	4
.90	21	12	7	5	4
.95	23	14	9	7	4
.99	*	20	13	8	6

*Well over 30 informants needed.

competence level of .6 one needs 9 informants in order to classify correctly at least 90% of the questions at the .95 confidence level.

The important point to observe is that small samples can yield extremely reliable data. Reliability of aggregated responses is not just a function of sample size, but is also a function of the agreement among informants. Are we really justified in using as few as a half-dozen subjects with only a few dozen items? We feel that the answer is yes, because there now exists a formal theory with clearly defined assumptions assuring us that when we are interviewing about culture patterns or items with high agreement, reliable and valid answers can be obtained with small numbers of informants.

Summary

When interest is primarily focused upon how well items with known answers classify individuals as to ability levels, then traditional item reliability is appropriate. When interest focuses on how well informants are reporting on cultural or social information and on estimating what that information is, then consensus analysis is appropriate. Either type of analysis is applicable to data from any of the interview formats.

Although item reliability may be applied to any structured data format, multiple-choice questions are used most frequently. Achievement and aptitude tests are constructed principally from multiple-choice questions. Informants' responses to such questions are recoded to correct/incorrect prior to analysis of item reliability. Overall reliability of test *items* an be calculated from the average intercorrelation among items (across all respondents) and the number of items. An item's reliability can be calculated by correlating the responses for that item with the sum of all items (item-to-total correlation).

The consensus model is conceptually similar to a reliability of people instead of items. It can be applied to dichotomous or multiple-choice data (Romney, Weller, and Batchelder, 1986) as well as rank ordered data (Romney, Batchelder, and Weller, 1987). Rating scales can be considered as multiple-choice or ranked data. Consensus analysis can be approximated by using an aggregation of raw responses as the best estimate of the answers and correlating each individual's responses to that aggregation (person-to-total correlation; Romney and Weller, 1984; Weller, 1984b; Weller, Romney, and Orr, 1987; Weller, 1987). Reliability of the aggregate can be estimated from the average intercorrelation among *respondents* and the number of respondents (Weller, 1987). The same logic can be applied to any data format.

12. VALIDITY AND REPLICATION WITH VARIATIONS

In this final chapter we turn our attention to the topic of validity, namely, how we know we are measuring what we think we are measuring. The aim of research is to produce results that are valid and robust. By that we generally mean that the results reflect the meanings intended by the researcher and that they would stand up under a variety of circumstances. In order to validate findings it is usually necessary to look beyond the results of a single study and to compare the results from the single study to additional studies and criteria. The criteria for reliability, discussed in the last chapter, are primarily based on internal consistency in the data. The criteria for validity include comparisons to information external to the original data.

Replication of a study under different circumstances is closely related to the concept of validity. To the extent that studies replicate, evidence accumulates, providing confidence in the validity of the results. Similarly, if different approaches are used to test the same concept and each method produces concordant results, then confidence in the validity of the measures increases. A triangulation of methodologic approaches is important in discovering true relationships. In this chapter we first discuss the technical meaning of validity and then discuss various strategies of replication with variations. The application of these methods ultimately determines how much confidence we can place in the results of our studies.

Traditional Approaches to Validity

Many researchers distinguish three types of validity: (1) content, (2) criterion related, and (3) construct validity (Carmines and Zeller, 1979; Nunnally, 1978). The first, content or face validity, is "built in" by the investigator when there is a priori agreement that the content reflects the desired objectives of the measurement instrument. The second, predictive validity, refers to a close relationship between the results of a measuring instrument and some a priori agreed upon external criterion. The measuring instrument (constructed from the use of one or other of the formats presented earlier) is said to "predict" the criterion. The third, construct validity, refers to the consistency among items that are supposed to measure "the same thing," namely, the constructed concept, for example, intelligence. Each of these kinds of validity will be elaborated on below.

The first and most intuitive kind of validity is content validity. Here, an attempt is made to ensure the validity of the instrument at the level of planning and constructing the instrument, rather than testing the validity of the measures after construction. Most classroom examinations depend solely upon content validity. Teachers construct tests based on material that was covered in class and thus the test should measure what the student learned in the class. Achievement tests also are judged in part on the basis of their content validity.

Content validity answers the simple question, Does the test (or interview) make sense? For example, since we know that prestige is one dimension in the perception of occupations, it would "make sense" to have informants order (with rating scales or ranking tasks) occupations in terms of their relative prestige. Similarly, discriminations of similarity / dissimilarity seem basic in any culture, so tasks in which subjects are asked to differentiate items based upon their relative similarity (e.g., triads or pile sort similarity data) would have high content validity. Ranking occupations in terms of their color or size would have questionable content validity. Content validity is ensured by the "naturalness" and "sensibleness" of the data collection task.

Content validity tends to break down when items come from more than one domain or if they are not all at the same "level of contrast." Ordering a mixed set of household utensils and modes of transportation on their relative usefulness does not "make sense" as much as ordering the items within each set or domain separately. Similarly, when items are not all at the same level of contrast, that is, they represent different levels of generic relations among items in a set (robin, eagle, blackbird, bird, animal), content validity is weakened.

A second type of validity is predictive or criterion validity. In predictive validity, items, tests, or interviews are used to predict an external criterion. For example, can a questionnaire for alcoholism differentiate known alcoholics from nonalcoholics? If questions are being used as a proxy for some behavior, can those questions predict actual behavior?

Methodological studies are very important in establishing the validity of data collection techniques under different conditions. Especially important are studies that compare reports with real world criteria. When informants' estimates of distances were collected using a variety of methods (including triad similarity judgments and estimates of distances), the data correlated highly with actual distances (Magaña et al., 1981). When informants estimated the height of their colleagues (using rating scales) the estimated heights correlated well with actual height (Dawes, 1977). Informants' rank ordering of causes of death correlated highly with the actual numbers of death due to each cause (Romney, Batchelder, and Weller, 1987).

One must be careful, however, in assuming that the criterion also is valid. With height and distances we can be relatively safe in assuming that the measurements of actual distances are not biased in any systematic way. Comparisons of reported behavior and observed behavior oftentimes have assumed that the observed behavior is somehow error free and represents the "truth." This is, of course, not true as many behaviors and interactions are not observable and people may be reporting over some aggregated time period that is different from the sampling frame for the behavioral observations. In a series of very creative experiments, Bernard et al. (1980) collected reports of social interactions (rating scales and ranking tasks) and compared those reports to behavioral observations of interactions. Although these researchers concluded that there is no relation between what people say they do and what they do, new studies have shown that informants' reports represent what they *usually* do (Freeman et al., 1987).

The third type of validity may be referred to as construct validity. This is by far the most abstract form of validation. It may be defined as consisting of three steps. First, one defines several different ways of measuring the same concept or "construct" of interest. Second, the interrelations among the various ways of measuring a construct are compared. Items measuring the same construct should be concordant. Finally, theoretical predictions among constructs can be hypothesized and tested with controlled experiments or carefully designed observations.

We can illustrate construct validity by reporting a series of studies on the semantic structure of animal terms. The construct under consideration is the notion that each of us carries around in our heads something that is isomorphic to the semantic structure of the domain of animals. Each animal has an appropriate location in that space. Animals that are judged as similar to each other are close together in the space, animals that are judged as dissimilar to each other are further apart in the space. An example of a representation of such a semantic structure is the fruit and vegetable example in Chapter 2.

Henley (1969: 176-184) used five different techniques to measure the semantic similarities among animals. She used free listing, pair rating, triads, verbal associations, and paired associate learning. The first procedure that Henley (1969: 177) used was the free listing task in which "subjects were asked to list all the animals they could within 10 min." Note that our recommendation that free listing come early in a study is exemplified in this study. Henley notes that the frequency with which an animal is named is related to its frequency of use in the language in general. The log frequencies from the Thorndike and Lorge (1944) word-frequency count correlated .57 with her observed frequencies. She computed the similarity between animals for each of the data collection techniques. From a careful comparison of the various results she concluded that:

> The supposition that the field of animal terms is highly structured is valid. The four experiments that successfully investigated the animal semantic structure found varying degrees of organization. The reliability measures

> used in the scaling experiments indicate that the semantic structure is in general quite stable [1969: 183].

Two very important laboratory experiments followed on the basis of Henley. One by Rumelhart and Abrahamson (1973) demonstrated that the semantic structure as measured by Henley would predict the performance on a set of analogy problems. Thus the measures related to a theoretical hypothesis that could be tested in an experiment. The second study by Hutchinson and Lockhead (1977) demonstrated that the semantic structure could be used to predict how difficult different judgments of similarity among subsets of animals were as indexed by reaction time. Here was a further theoretical hypothesis that could be tested in an experiment. Taken all together these studies provide powerful evidence that there is a semantic structure and that it affects cognitive functions such as solving analogies and the length of time to solve similarity judgments.

Let's review why the above example fits the criteria for construct validity. First, the domain specified for the study was the semantic structure among animal names. Second, the various ways of measuring the similarity among animal names were all interrelated. Third, the studies involving experiments demonstrated that theoretically derived predictions involving the constructs relation to outside variables (solution of analogies and reaction time) were borne out in actual experiments. We note that construct validity involves several studies and may involve different researchers. The evidence is built up over time, is highly abstract, but at some point becomes quite convincing.

Some Final Remarks on Replication Studies

In this book we have shown how a researcher can define a domain of interest using free lists. We then reviewed a number of ways of collecting data about the domain. Finally, we have introduced the concepts of reliability and validity to demonstrate that structured interviewing results can be valid and can be replicated. In the discussion of the various ways of collecting data we have commented on some of the advantages and disadvantages of the various methods. We now turn to the question as to whether or not the choice of format would make a sizable difference in determining the outcome of a study. If we are interested in collecting judged similarity among a number of objects, for example, fruits, colors, and animals, would we get different results depending upon the choice of data collection format? A related question is whether or not slight changes in the instructions might have a big effect.

If the choice of data collection format or changes in the wording of instructions have major effects on the outcome of the research then our research task is enormously complicated. On the other hand, if the same results can be obtained from a variety of data collection formats using reasonable variations in directions then stable and robust research generalizations should be easier to obtain. Despite a few genuine exceptions, the majority of the evidence indicates that most results are stable over a variety of formats and wording variations. We review some of the relevant studies below.

One of the more ambitious studies of variations in formats and directions was carried out by Miller (1974). He collected judged similarity data on 15 personality traits using six different data collection formats. He also tested three differently worded sets of directions for each of the formats. This resulted in 18 separate experimental groups. The three sets of directions differed as follows: The first set stressed similarity in terms of items "most similar in meaning." The second set stressed similarity in terms of items "you might expect to find together." The third set stressed similarity in terms of items "you feel belong together." Similarity data were collected with triads and five different variations of the pile sort.

Miller found that all 18 situations produced virtually the same picture of the structure of personality terms. From his data we calculated the reliability of informants in groups of size 12 to be .92 and in groups of size 6 the average reliability was .86. Insofar as could be detected by an analysis of the results, there were no differences related to choice of data collection method or wording of directions. The only detectable difference was that reliability was better for large groups rather than small groups of informants. These findings are encouraging and increase confidence that measures obtained from structured interviews are stable and can be replicated.

In a similar study reported by Friendly (1979) five formats were used to test for clusters of animal names.

> Three groups of subjects were tested. One group (Group A1; N = 78) was asked to list up to 50 animals. Following this, they were asked to sort the items they had produced into an arbitrary number of categories, based on "similarity." The 24 most frequently emitted words were selected and a second group (A2; N = 33) merely sorted these into subjective categories. A third group (A3; N = 16) was engaged in a free-recall task with six trials, followed by a sorting task in which they were asked to group together words that tended to go together in their recall.

When proximity measures for each of the five tasks were clustered using hierarchical clustering the correspondence across tasks was striking. The correlations among solutions derived from the various tasks ranged between .78 and .91. This means that the results from the variety of tasks were all virtually the same. Each task was measuring the "same" thing with a high degree of reliability.

Summary

The usefulness of collecting systematic interview data from subjects has been recognized for many years. We feel that ever more powerful applications will be found for such methods in the next several years. It is our hope that the methods outlined in this book will contribute to such developments. We will review some of the more salient highlights.

The choice of the domain of study is appropriately based upon the interests of the individual researcher. The free-listing task, with appropriate modifications for special situations, can be of great help in defining and determining the items to be included in the study. The use of the free-listing task ensures that the domain is defined by the informants and not imposed by the researcher. It also ensures that the domain is coherent, that the items are at the same level of contrast, and that the informants are acquainted with the items.

It is important in the planning stages of any research to define clearly the focus of the study and the main research questions. The choice of what question format to use, for example, depends upon whether the focus is on individual differences among informants or on describing similarities and differences among items or objects. Other considerations in the choice of format selection include the number of objects in the domain, whether the informants are literate or nonliterate, and the amount of prior knowledge the researcher has regarding the informants and their culture. In the various chapters we have indicated the possible advantages and disadvantages of each format in terms of these considerations.

Each different research context may require a different choice of interview or data collection format. We have presented a variety of formats for consideration. Each format is described with sufficient detail to facilitate its use in the construction of a research instrument. Strong and weak points for each format are outlined to make it possible to choose an appropriate format for each research context. Information on balanced incomplete block designs is included to extend the range of appreciation of some of the formats (triad and ranking).

The appropriate use of the methods presented in the book can be expected to produce results that are reliable and valid. In the areas that the methods have been applied the results have been very gratifying. We feel that the implications of the last two chapters are particularly noteworthy. The development of the theory of reliability and test theory during the last century is one of the major contributions of the social sciences. Consensus theory may be seen as extending the logic of reliability to the study of informant consistency.

Reliability and consensus may be seen as ways of checking on the internal coherence among sets of items or groups of people. Reliability allows one to infer from internal consistency criteria whether the items are all measuring a similar attribute or trait of individuals. Consensus allows one to infer from similar criteria whether informants are reporting on the same cultural information. The main theme of both is that the data collected have some internal coherence that gives the researcher increased confidence that the data are consistent.

The last chapter turns to the question of validity. The study of validity, as we have seen, generally relates to the interrelations among a series of variables, some of which are external to the data collected in a single study. A triangulation of different methods with convergent results assures construct validity. It is the most abstract type of validity and is generally regarded as the most useful kind.

We hope that these various methods and data collection formats will be found helpful. We are convinced that improvements are possible in the quality of much of social science research through the application of the principles outlined here. Careful attention to domain definition, to choice of data collection format, and to the use of reliability, consensus, and validity concepts should improve the overall quality of research.

APPENDIX A
Random Numbers

30327	18630	50546	66082	41159	13769	69069	98638	78132	89538	76499	07762
64274	43724	09355	95905	69762	61880	27973	33864	58883	27749	24279	96874
52933	23102	68353	73543	39262	95359	15207	34248	72167	78690	44926	10234
99814	52582	88678	52288	06399	89836	39795	25021	89157	10896	80219	31220
10839	96272	18566	71901	05841	86756	83596	72543	00415	93504	28442	99089
64532	28043	50186	97891	46841	47915	60099	46086	51850	98324	03459	88883
79369	56944	72950	96578	23520	59823	18115	19043	77052	05354	16622	13489
72473	18311	07590	41773	74186	76260	77228	41641	25009	67033	75902	08062
06636	31445	70284	28510	58351	79903	38862	66538	81912	62540	33253	36275
14542	14401	59741	18269	68473	00089	56795	89496	71563	25054	37607	32433
97264	30998	86509	05592	27533	73713	36500	31583	70693	16205	60212	98391
48304	13561	61015	55500	34097	95897	47526	60599	80484	67998	75364	89855
44050	25991	24140	98786	59568	69527	77301	35688	12901	95838	13636	75538
61927	12986	56083	58176	96857	76473	55149	48214	57438	04245	04760	82538
67278	02794	59883	81342	25203	74719	58920	62413	64613	28324	75909	05819
51232	71654	62291	86512	38261	68726	80823	44703	61216	40650	86571	31293
76008	18571	70444	50997	41898	97275	45214	75034	93415	79833	30986	25380
53457	92759	15692	40749	20252	94374	32165	85560	72065	91110	91093	43358
02064	42003	29082	66895	46284	60962	81016	42875	39296	73757	47712	59994
96189	93080	72408	50326	21036	67021	66129	05168	72255	46507	40295	82526
60096	18267	88451	20780	13376	86668	37511	77393	45213	54311	41379	46401
92126	74740	62446	49825	03170	07455	80177	07330	82473	86672	14009	91144
27529	41624	97142	03527	40490	82516	26105	23749	90809	85200	76387	71039
28416	05879	41462	72666	13340	46835	82130	89467	59123	49790	06486	10759
88913	26034	01297	81988	63710	52088	28572	78239	69020	17901	05184	21165
67587	21470	75583	30475	79729	82931	83741	80164	87779	20366	96277	69796
26517	06828	85161	01052	56508	65644	68683	40747	70616	74203	76242	32994
43848	96986	41837	47235	28638	73600	29431	03206	18655	22372	93589	53032

APPENDIX B
Internal Randomization of Triads

6	3	2	5	3
5	5	3	1	6
4	1	6	5	3
5	3	6	6	3
4	4	1	6	4
5	1	3	2	5
1	2	6	4	2
3	5	5	2	5
5	6	2	3	1
1	6	1	3	6
6	3	6	2	2
3	1	4	5	5
4	4	3	4	4
6	1	6	1	3
2	6	2	1	6
6	2	4	5	4
4	5	1	5	2
3	3	4	3	4
2	5	1	6	5
4	1	2	4	3

Orders

1 = 1 2 3
2 = 1 3 2
3 = 2 1 3
4 = 2 3 1
5 = 3 1 2
6 = 3 2 1

APPENDIX C
Triad Design
(15 items, 3 per block, 70 blocks, each pair appears twice)

3	11	14	12	1	7	15	2	3
9	1	15	4	9	1	1	15	12
3	9	6	3	1	8	8	13	2
11	13	6	7	6	10	8	4	15
4	11	13	14	8	10	13	9	8
13	14	15	2	8	6	15	11	9
2	12	14	14	10	6	4	2	7
11	4	10	12	2	13	12	13	9
6	1	14	6	15	2	12	11	8
14	1	4	15	5	12	11	8	14
5	1	11	4	15	6	8	9	7
4	7	8	5	13	3	10	3	8
11	5	7	13	7	6	5	4	6

(continued)

Appendix C continued

6	5	9	14	9	2	13	7	1
12	8	6	1	2	3	7	11	2
14	15	7	1	8	5	2	11	9
10	2	5	7	5	12	1	6	11
4	12	3	15	5	8	15	10	7
15	10	13	10	9	4	10	2	1
4	5	2	5	14	13	12	4	14
3	7	14	9	3	7	9	10	12
1	13	10	10	11	12	5	14	9
11	3	15	3	10	5	3	13	4
6	12	3						

APPENDIX D
Triad Design
(19 items, 3 per block, 57 blocks, each pair appears once)

18	9	3	16	7	1	9	13	19
17	7	11	15	12	10	16	13	11
6	4	9	4	16	5	4	2	7
1	8	9	14	17	12	5	11	1
2	17	8	9	2	10	12	8	18
13	8	10	2	16	18	5	6	17
14	2	3	14	16	19	19	4	10
19	5	2	6	3	1	14	5	18
5	13	12	9	11	14	8	19	7
10	16	6	17	1	15	4	3	15
8	5	3	3	12	16	8	16	15
19	3	17	18	19	11	11	15	2
9	5	15	3	10	11	7	9	12
19	15	6	13	15	18	12	2	6
18	4	1	6	7	18	15	14	7
11	6	8	9	16	17	11	4	12
18	10	17	13	6	14	4	14	8
17	4	13	1	12	19	10	1	14
7	13	3	1	13	2	10	5	7

APPENDIX E

Triad Design

(21 items, 3 per block, 70 blocks, each pair appears once)

13	19	1	6	7	18	21	12	13
20	5	18	17	19	4	11	12	10
5	14	8	4	9	13	21	9	5
2	5	11	19	18	2	18	16	17
17	10	9	16	21	6	2	4	14
21	20	19	19	12	7	19	14	3
7	14	17	1	7	21	11	15	20
5	10	13	21	2	15	20	3	4
12	15	6	11	6	14	14	1	16
3	17	15	13	3	6	1	6	9
14	9	20	16	4	12	13	16	11
17	1	5	15	5	7	4	6	5
7	20	13	12	20	1	11	7	3
3	2	1	21	18	4	11	21	17
1	4	15	18	10	3	9	16	3
2	10	20	14	15	13	10	4	7
7	9	8	15	8	19	9	2	12
13	8	18	1	8	10	10	16	15
16	7	2	16	20	8	17	2	13
16	19	5	8	2	6	12	8	17
10	19	6	5	12	3	6	17	20
18	14	12	19	9	11	18	11	1
14	21	10	4	11	8	8	21	3
9	18	15						

APPENDIX F

(13 items, 4 per block, 13 blocks, each pair appears once)

3	6	10	11	9	4	7	11	3	13	9	5
10	13	7	2	2	8	5	11	8	13	6	4
1	12	11	13	4	5	10	12	8	3	7	12
2	9	12	6	6	5	7	1	8	9	10	1
3	4	1	2								

APPENDIX G

(21 items, 5 per block, 21 blocks, each pair appears once)

19	6	16	4	20	8	3	2	20	10	15	5	19	3	18
13	18	9	20	12	1	8	18	21	6	3	7	6	12	14
15	20	14	1	11	12	16	2	15	21	8	5	9	14	16
18	2	4	17	14	6	13	2	11	5	13	10	19	14	21
16	17	1	13	3	9	3	21	4	11	18	7	16	10	11
17	20	21	7	5	19	8	12	17	11	15	17	10	9	6
4	8	15	7	13	1	10	4	12	5	7	2	1	19	9

APPENDIX H

(25 items, 5 per block, 30 blocks, each pair appears once)

7	22	5	12	16	8	14	4	23	24	3	21	6	11	15
12	11	10	14	19	8	5	13	17	6	15	5	23	9	10
4	16	1	10	6	21	8	2	10	22	6	23	12	2	25
19	18	4	5	21	12	15	4	20	13	22	15	14	17	1
11	9	16	20	8	15	16	2	18	24	9	7	14	18	6
17	11	2	7	4	20	17	18	10	25	8	25	15	7	19
18	3	12	1	8	3	23	16	17	19	9	24	17	12	21
6	22	24	20	19	2	13	1	19	9	25	5	11	24	1
5	20	14	2	3	21	1	23	7	20	16	14	21	13	25
24	13	3	7	10	3	9	22	4	25	18	23	11	22	13

APPENDIX I

(31 items, 6 per block, 31 blocks, each pair appears once)

30	6	16	10	1	29	20	25	18	29	4	17	13	30	12	15	20	24
12	22	16	4	5	7	31	12	3	1	18	8	19	4	13	1	9	2
9	18	6	14	24	7	21	20	7	23	1	28	9	22	30	23	25	3
13	23	5	8	6	17	27	8	14	30	4	28	30	11	2	31	17	7
20	11	8	26	16	9	21	10	12	27	17	9	11	19	14	29	23	12
25	13	31	21	16	14	29	27	13	3	7	26	16	19	24	3	17	28
6	25	12	28	2	26	11	28	10	22	13	18	28	15	5	29	9	31
19	31	20	27	6	22	10	20	5	2	3	14	21	24	2	29	22	8
24	10	31	4	26	23	18	21	26	5	19	30	25	7	10	19	8	15
4	3	21	6	11	15	1	22	17	15	14	26	11	1	24	27	25	5
23	27	16	15	2	18												

REFERENCES

ARABIE, P. and S. A. BOORMAN (1973) "Multidimensional scaling of measures of distances between partitions." J. of Mathematical Psychology 10: 148-203.

BATCHELDER, W. H. and A. K. ROMNEY (1986) "The statistical analysis of a general condorcet model for dichotomous choice situations," in B. Grofman and G. Owen (eds.) Information Pooling and Group Decision Making. CT: JAI.

BERLIN, B. and A. K. ROMNEY (1964) "Some semantic implications of Tzeltal numeral classifiers." Amer. Anthropologist Special Issue 66, 3: 79-98.

BOORMAN, S. A. and P. ARABIE (1972) "Structural measures and the method of sorting," in R. Shepard et al. (eds.) Multidimensional Scaling: Theory and Applications in the Behavioral Sciences, Vol. I. New York: Seminar Press.

BOORMAN, S. A. and D. C. OLIVIER (1973) "Metrics on spaces of finite trees." J. of Mathematical Psychology 10: 26-59.

BOSTER, J. S. (1985) "Requiem for the omniscient informant: there's life in the old girl yet," pp. 177-197 in J. Dougherty (ed.) Directions in Cognitive Anthropology. Urbana: Univ. of Illinois Press.

BOSTER, J. S. (1986a) "Can individuals recapitulate the evolutionary development of color lexicons." Ethnology 25, 1: 61-74.

BOSTER, J. S. (1986b) "Exchange of varieties and information between Aquaruna manioc cultivators." Amer. Anthropologist 88: 428-436.

BRUNER, J., J. J. GOODNOW, and G. A. AUSTIN (1965) A Study of Thinking. New York: Science Editions.

BURTON, M. L. (1968) "Multidimensional scaling of role terms." University Microfilms, No. 69-8106.

BURTON, M. L. (1972) "Semantic dimensions of occupation names." pp. 55-77 in A. K. Romney et al. (eds.) Multidimensional Scaling: Theory and Applications in the Behavioral Sciences, Vol. 2. New York: Seminar Press.

BURTON, M. L. (1975) "Dissimilarity measures for unconstrained sorting data." Multivariate Behavioral Research 10: 409-424.

BURTON, M. L. and L. KIRK (1979) "Sex differences in Maasai cognition of personality and social identity." Amer. Anthropology 81: 841-873.

BURTON, M. L. and S. B. NERLOVE (1976) "Balanced designs for triads tests: two examples from English." Social Sci. Research 5: 247-267.

BURTON, M. L. and A. K. ROMNEY (1975) "A multidimensional representation of role terms." Amer. Ethnologist 2, 3: 397-407.

CLIFF, N. (1959) "Adverbs as multipliers." Psych. Rev. 66: 27-44.

DAHLSTROM, W. G., G. S. WELSH, and L. E. DAHLSTROM (1975) An MMPI Handbook, Vol. 2: Research Applications. Minneapolis: Univ. of Minnesota Press.

D'ANDRADE, R. G. (1976) "A propositional analysis of U.S. American beliefs about illness," in K. H. Basso and H. Selby (eds.) Meaning in Anthropology.

D'ANDRADE, R. G. (1978) "U-statistic clustering." Psychometrika 43, 1: 59-67.

D'ANDRADE, R. G., N. QUINN, S. B. NERLOVE, and A. K. ROMNEY (1972) "Categories of disease in American-English and Mexican-Spanish," pp. 9-54 in A. K. Romney et al. (eds.) Multidimensional Scaling: Theory and Applications in the Behavioral Sciences, Vol. 2. New York: Seminar Press.

DAWES, R. M. (1977) "Suppose we measured height with rating scales instead of rulers." Applied Psych. Measurement 1, 1: 267-273.

FABREGA, H. Jr. (1970) "On the specificity of folk illnesses." Southwestern J. of Anthropology 26: 305-314.

FILLENBAUM, S. and A. RAPOPORT (1971) Structures in the Subjective Lexicon. New York: Academic Press.

FOSTER, G. M. (1979) "Brief communications." Human Organization 38, 2: 179-183.

FREEMAN, H. E., A. K. ROMNEY, J. FERREIRA-PINTO, R. E. KLEIN, and T. SMITH (1981) "Guatemalan and U.S. concepts of success and failure." Human Organization 40, 2: 140-145.

FREEMAN, L., S. FREEMAN and A. MICHAELSON (1986) "Group structure and the perception of groups." Social Network Meetings, Clearwater, Florida

FREEMAN, L. C., A. K. ROMNEY, and S. C. FREEMAN (1987) "Cognitive structure and informant accuracy." Amer. Anthropologist 89, 2: 310-325.

FREY, J. H. (1983) Survey Research by Telephone. Newbury Park, CA: Sage.

FRIENDLY, M. L. (1977) "In search of the M-gram: the structure of organization in free recall." Cognitive Psychology 9: 188-249.

FRIENDLY, M. L. (1979) "Methods for finding graphic representations of associative memory structure," pp. 85-129 in C. R. Puff (ed.) Memory Organization and Structure. New York: Academic Press.

GARRO, L. C. (1986) "Intracultural variation in folk medical knowledge: a comparison between curers and noncurers." Amer. Anthropologist 88, 2: 351-370.

GARRO, L. C. (1987) "Explaining high bood pressure: variation in knowledge about illness." Amer. Ethnologist.

GREEN, P. E. and F. J. CARMONE (1970) Multidimensional Scaling and Related Techniques in Marketing Analysis. Boston: Allyn & Bacon.

GUILFORD, J. P. (1954) Psychometric Methods. New York: Maple.

GULLIKSEN, H. and L. R. TUCKER (1961) "A general procedure for obtaining paired-comparisons from multiple rank orders." Psychometrika 26, 2: 173-183.

HALL, M. Jr. (1967) Combinatorial Theory. Waltham: Blaisdell.

HENLEY, N. M. (1969) "A Psychological Study of the Semantics of Animal Terms." J. of Verbal Learning and Verbal Behavior 8: 176-184.

HUTCHINSON, J. W. and G. R. LOCKHEAD (1977) "Similarity as distance: a structural principle for semantic memory." Human Learning and Memory, 6, 3: 660-678.

JOHNSON, J. C. and M. L. MILLER (1983) "Deviant social positions in small groups: the relations between role and individual." Social Networks 5: 51-69.

JOHNSON, S. C. (1967) "Hierarchical clustering schemes." Psychometrika 32: 241-254.

KIRK, J. and M. L. MILLER (1986) Reliability and Validity in Qualitative Research. Newbury Park, CA: Sage.

KIRK, L. and M. BURTON (1977) "Meaning and context: a study in contextual shifts in meaning of Maasai personality descriptors." Amer. Ethnologist 4, 4: 734-761.

KNUTH, D. E. (1973) Sorting and Searching. Reading: Addison Wesley.

KRACKHARDT, D. and KILDUFF (1987) "Diversity is strength: a social network approach to the constructs of organizational culture." Working paper, Johnson School of Management, Cornell.

LIEBERMAN, D. and W. M. DRESSLER (1977) "Bilingualism and cognition of St. Lucian disease terms." Medical Anthropology 1: 81-110.

LORD, F. M. and M. R. NOVICK (1968) Statistical Theories of Mental Test Scores.

MAGAÑA, J. R., G. W. EVANS, and A. K. ROMNEY (1981) "Scaling techniques in the analysis of environmental cognition data." Professional Geographer 33: 294-310.

MILLER, G. A. (1969) "A psychological method to investigate verbal concepts." J. of Mathematical Psychology 6: 169-191.

MILLER, M. L. (1974) "A comparison of judged-similarity, trait inference and trait rating tasks with regard to the multidimensional structure of personality traits." Ph.D. dissertation, University of California, Irvine.

MILLER, M. L. and J. C. JOHNSON (1981) "Hard work and competition in an Alaskan fishery." Human Organization.

NERLOVE, S. B. and A. S. WALTERS (1977) "Pooling intra-cultural variation: toward empirically based statements of community consensus." Ethnology 16: 427-441.

NUNNALLY, J. C. (1978) Psychometric Theory. New York: McGraw-Hill.

OSGOOD, C. E., W. H. MAY, and M. S. MIRON (1975) Cross-Cultural Universals of Affective Meaning. Urbana: Univ. of Illinois Press.

OSGOOD, C. E., G. J. SUCI, and P. TANNENBAUM (1957) The Measurement of Meaning. Urbana: Univ. of Illinois Press.

PERCHONOCK, N. and O. WERNER (1968) "Navaho systems of classification: some implications of ethnoscience." Ethnology 8: 229-243.

RIVERS, W.H.R. (1910) "The geneological method." Amer. Soc. Rev. 3: 1-11.

ROBERTS, F. S. (1985) "Applications of the theory of meaningfulness to psychology." J. of Mathematical Psychology 29: 311-332.

ROBERTS, J. M. and G. E. CHICK (1979) "Butler County eight ball: a behavioral space analysis." pp. 65-99 in J. H. Goldstein (ed.) Sports, Games, and Play: Social and Psychological Viewpoints. Hillsdale: Lawrence Erlbaum.

ROBERTS, J. M., G. E. CHICK, M. STEPHANSON, and L. L. HYDE (1981) "Inferred categories for tennis play: a limited semantic analysis," pp. 181-195 in A. B. Cheska (ed.) Play as Context. West Point: Leisure.

ROBERTS, J. M., T. V. GOLDER, and G. E. CHICK (1980) "Judgment, oversight and skill: a cultural analysis of P-3 pilot error." Human Organization 39, 1: 5-21.

ROBERTS, J. M. and S. H. NUTTRAS (1980) "Women and trapshooting: competence and expression in a game of skill with chance," pp. 262-291 in H. B. Schwartzman (ed.) Play and Culture. West Point: Leisure.

ROMNEY, A. K., W. H. BATCHELDER, and S. C. WELLER (1987) "Recent applications of consensus theory." Amer. Behav. Sci. 31(2): 163-177.

ROMNEY, A. K. and R. G. D'ANDRADE (1964) "Cognitive aspects of English kin terms." Amer. Anthropologist 66, 3: 146-170.

ROMNEY, A. K., M. KEIFFER, and R. E. KLEIN (1979) "A normalization procedure for correcting biased response data." Social Sci. Research 2: 307-320.

ROMNEY, A. K. and J. R. MAGAÑA (1977) "The reliability of cognitive structures across Spanish-English language boundaries." Presented at the National Anthropological Association Meeting, Houston.

ROMNEY, A. K., T. SMITH, H. E. FREEMAN, J. KAGAN, and R. E. KLEIN (1979) "Concepts of success and failure." Social Sci. Research 8: 302-326.

ROMNEY, A. K. and S. C. WELLER (1984) "Predicting informant accuracy from patterns of recall among individuals." Social Networks 4: 59-77.

ROMNEY, A. K., S. C. WELLER, and W. H. BATCHELDER (1986) "Culture as consensus: a theory of cultural and informant accuracy." Amer. Anthropologist 88, 2: 313-338.

ROSENBERG, S. and M. P. KIM (1975) "The method of sorting as a data-gathering procedure in multivariate research." Multivariate Behavioral Research 10: 489-502.

RUMELHART, D. E. and A. A. ABRAHAMSON (1973) "A model for analogical reasoning." Cognitive Psychology 5: 1-28.

SANKOFF, G. (1971) "Quantitative analysis of sharing and variability in a cognitive model." Ethnology 10: 389-408.

SNEATH, P.H.A. and R. R. SOKAL (1973) Numerical Taxonomy. San Francisco: W. H. Freeman.

SOGN, D. L. (1979) "The child with a lifethreatening illness: an analysis of the impact of experience on the awareness of personal mortality." Ph.D. disseration, University of California, Irvine.

SPSS, INC (1986) SPSS-X. New York: McGraw-Hill.

STEFFLRE, V. J. (1972) "Some applications of multidimensional scaling to social science problems," pp. 211-243 in A. K. Romney et al. (eds.) Multidimensional Scaling: Theory and Applications in the Behavioral Sciences, Vol. 2. New York: Academic Press.

STEFFLRE, V. J., P. REICH, and M. McCLARAN-STEFFLRE (1971) "Some eliciting and computational procedures for descriptive semantics," pp. 79-116 in P. Kay (ed.) Explorations in Mathematical Anthropology. Cambridge: MIT Press.

THORNDIKE, E. L. and I. LORGE (1944) The Teacher's Word Book of 30,000 Words. New York: Teachers College, Columbia University.

TRUEX, G. F. (1977) "Measurement of intersubject variations in categorizations." J. of Cross-Cultural Psychology 8, 1: 71-82.

WELLER, S. C. (1980) "A cross-cultural comparison of illness concepts: Guatemala and the United States." Ph.D. dissertation, University of California, Irvine.

WELLER, S. C. (1983) "New data on intra-cultural variation: the hot-cold concept." Human Organization 42: 249-257.

WELLER, S. C. (1984a) "Cross-cultural concepts of illness: variation and validation." Amer. Anthropologist 86: 341-351.

WELLER, S. C. (1984b) "Consistency and consensus among informants: disease concepts in a rural Mexican village." Amer. Anthropologist 86: 966-975.

WELLER, S. C. (1987) "Shared knowledge, intracultural variation and knowledge aggregation." Amer. Behavioral Scientist 31(2): 178-193.

WELLER, S. C. and C. H. BUCHHOLTZ (1986) "When a single clustering method creates more than one tree: a reanalysis of the Salish languages." Amer. Anthropologist 88: 667-674.

WELLER, S. C. and R. DOUGHTY (1985) "Measuring clinical competency among medical residents." Presented at Social Network meetings, Palm Beach, Florida.

WELLER, S. C. and C. I. DUNGY (1986) "Personal preferences and ethnic variations among Anglo and Hispanic breast and bottle feeders." Social Sci. and Medicine 23, 6: 539-548.

WELLER, S. C., A. K. ROMNEY, and D. P. ORR (1987) "The myth of a sub-culture of corporal punishment." Human Organization 46: 39-47.

WHITE, G. (1978) "Ambiguity and ambivalence in A'ra descriptors." Amer. Ethnologist 5: 334-360.

YOUNG, J. C. (1978) "Illness categories and action strategies in a Tarascan town." Amer. Ethnologist 5: 81-97.

YOUNG, J. C. (1980) "A model of illness treatment decisions in a Tarascan town." Amer. Ethnologist 7, 1: 106-131.

YOUNG, J. C. and L. C. GARRO (1982) "Variation in the choice of treatment in two Mexican communities." Social Sci. and Medicine 16: 1453-1465.

ABOUT THE AUTHORS

SUSAN C. WELLER, Ph.D., is an Assistant Professor at the University of Pennsylvania in the Departments of Pediatrics, Clinical Epidemiology, and the Graduate Group of Anthropology. She is an anthropologist and methodologist specializing in the measurement of beliefs and attitudes. She is concerned with issues of intracultural variation, informant accuracy, and how we know when we have the "right" answers. The Cultural Consensus Model, developed with Romney and Batchelder, estimates informant accuracy and cultural belief. This monograph is intended as an easy-to-read handbook for researchers interested in studying attitudes and beliefs.

A. KIMBALL ROMNEY is Professor of Mathematical Social Science at the University of California, Irvine. His special interests include measurement and modeling in the social sciences with special reference to cognitive anthropology. Together with Roger Shepard and Sarah Nerlove he edited a pioneering two volume work on Multidimensional Scaling (1972, Seminar Press). More recently, he has written a series of articles on consensus theory with Batchelder and Weller. He has taught at Chicago, Harvard, and Stanford and has over 60 publications to his credit.

Printed in the United States
95261LV00002B/51/A